Potluck
family favorites

Cheesy Ham Strata, page 109

Potluck
family favorites

Oxmoor
House®

Potluck
family favorites

©2013 by Gooseberry Patch
2500 Farmers Dr., #110, Columbus, Ohio 43235
1-800-854-6673, **gooseberrypatch.com**
©2013 by Time Home Entertainment Inc.
135 West 50th Street, New York, NY 10020

ISBN-13: 978-0-8487-0582-4
ISBN-10: 0-8487-0582-3
Library of Congress Control Number: 2013930736
Printed in the United States of America
First Printing 2013

Oxmoor House
Editorial Director: Leah McLaughlin
Creative Director: Felicity Keane
Brand Manager: Vanessa Tiongson
Senior Editor: Rebecca Brennan
Managing Editor: Rebecca Benton

Gooseberry Patch Potluck Family Favorites
Editor: Nichole Aksamit
Art Director: Claire Cormany
Assistant Designer: Allison Sperando Potter
Director, Test Kitchen: Elizabeth Tyler Austin
Assistant Directors, Test Kitchen: Julie Christopher, Julie Gunter
Recipe Developers and Testers: Wendy Ball, R.D.; Victoria E. Cox; Tamara Goldis; Stefanie Maloney; Callie Nash; Karen Rankin; Leah Van Deren
Recipe Editor: Alyson Moreland Haynes
Food Stylists: Margaret Monroe Dickey, Catherine Crowell Steele
Photography Director: Jim Bathie
Senior Photographer: Helene Dujardin
Senior Photo Stylist: Kay E. Clarke
Photo Stylist: Mindi Shapiro Levine
Assistant Photo Stylist: Mary Louise Menendez
Associate Production Manager: Kimberly Marshall
Assistant Production Manager: Diane Rose Keener

Contributors
Project Editor: Lacie Pinyan
Copy Editors: Norma Butterworth-McKittrick, Jasmine Hodges
Proofreader: Rhonda Lee Lother
Indexer: Mary Ann Laurens
Interns: Megan Branagh, Frances Gunnells, Susan Kemp, Sara Lyon, Staley McIlwain, Jeffrey Preis, Emily Robinson, Maria Sanders, Julia Sayers
Photographers: Becky Luigart-Stayner, Mary Britton Senseney, Daniel Taylor
Photo Stylists: Mary Clayton Carl, Missie Crawford, Anna Pollock, Leslie Simpson, Caitlin Van Horn

Time Home Entertainment Inc.
Publisher: Jim Childs
VP, Strategy & Business Development: Steven Sandonato
Executive Director, Marketing Services: Carol Pittard
Executive Director, Retail & Special Sales: Tom Mifsud
Director, Bookazine Development & Marketing: Laura Adam
Executive Publishing Director: Joy Butts
Associate Publishing Director: Megan Pearlman
Finance Director: Glenn Buonocore
Associate General Counsel: Helen Wan

To order additional publications, call 1-800-765-6400.
To search, savor, and share thousands of recipes, visit
myrecipes.com

Cover: Slow-Cooker Farmhouse Pot Roast (page 78)
Page 1: Triple Fudge Cake (page 261)

Country Apple Sipper,
page 10

Buttermilk Fried Chicken, page 61

Peanut Butter Pie, page 253

contents

Nana's Slow-Cooker Meatballs, page 42

Creamy Turkey Lasagna, page 103

Dear Friend,

We're having a potluck. Please join us! Aren't invitations like that music to your ears? Here at Gooseberry Patch, we love potlucks because they're a terrific way to bring friends, neighbors, co-workers & families together. They're also decidedly easy to host. Plus, when everyone brings a favorite dish to share, we all have more time to catch up.

That's why we're so pleased to bring you *Potluck Family Favorites*. This collection features everything you need for a great meal or a great…potluck, plus edible gifts you'll love to share. We've selected 200 delicious homestyle favorites from our kitchens and from those of the Gooseberry Patch family.

Any potluck will get off to a great start with Citrus Slush (page 14), Artichoke-Garlic Dip (page 18) or everyone's favorite…Nana's Slow-Cooker Meatballs (page 42). Main dishes are the mainstay of the supper table and the buffet, and with our easy entrées and casseroles, there's no need to stress. For a quick Italian fix, whip up Easy Cheesy Manicotti (page 46) or colorful Zesty Pizza Casserole (page 112). Don't want to turn on the oven or fire up the grill? Turn a few boiled eggs into a platter of delightful Dilly Egg Salad Sandwiches (page 141) or get out a grill pan and transform ground beef into juicy Grilled Garlic Burgers (page 81).

Don't forget the sides! A fresh Summer Vegetable Salad (page 160) is a great addition to any cookout, and Paula's Twice-Baked Potatoes (page 192) are always a favorite. Satisfy a sweet tooth with fluffy Peanut Butter Pie (page 253), and treat your host with a thoughtful gift, such as our delectable Carrot Cake Mix (page 290). These scrumptious, satisfying recipes answer two of life's most important and frequently asked questions: "What's for supper tonight?" and "What are you bringing?"

From our families to yours,

Vickie & JoAnn

sweet sips & noshable nibbles

Whether you're headed to a neighborhood potluck or hosting friends at home, stop here first for delectable drink and appetizer recipes. Citrus Slush (page 14) makes enough for a crowd, and the Tomato Cocktail (page 17) hits the spot for a weekend brunch. Get the party started with Oniony Crab Dip (page 29) or Scrumptious Stuffed Potato Skins (page 32). Make some Pizza Roll Snacks (page 37) for the kids and don't forget Glazed Cocktail Sausages (page 41)...a classic party snack!

Country Apple Sipper

(pictured on page 8)

A cinnamon stick makes a fun stirrer for this refreshing drink.

8 cinnamon herb teabags
1 qt. boiling water
12-oz. can frozen apple juice
    concentrate

1 apple, cored and sliced
6 6-inch cinnamon sticks

Add teabags to boiling water; steep 5 minutes. Remove and discard teabags; add apple juice concentrate to tea. Fill apple juice can 3 times with cold water and pour into tea mixture. Serve over ice in tall glasses. Add apple slices and cinnamon sticks. Serves 4 to 6.

Spiced Lemonade

Serve in frosted glasses with a skewer of fresh fruit.

6 6-inch cinnamon sticks
1 t. whole allspice

2 c. water
1 qt. fresh lemonade

Place cinnamon sticks and allspice in a saucepan; cover with water and simmer 10 minutes. Strain into a heatproof pitcher; discard cinnamon sticks and allspice. Add lemonade to cooking liquid; stir well and chill. Serves 6.

get out the punch bowl

For a dramatic presentation, double the recipe and serve this spiced lemonade in a punch bowl with a fruit-laced ice ring. Add citrus slices to a ring mold and pour water to partially cover the fruit. When frozen, add more water so that fruit is completely covered. Freeze again. To serve, carefully remove ice ring, place in punch bowl and pour spiced lemonade on top.

Fruity Spiced Tea

Enliven a grey day with this delicious and colorful blend of fruit juices and spices.

6 c. boiling water
1 T. unsweetened instant tea mix
½ t. allspice
½ t. cinnamon
½ t. nutmeg
3-oz. pkg. cherry gelatin mix

1 c. orange juice
¼ c. lemon juice
4 c. cranberry juice cocktail
½ c. sugar
Garnish: orange slices

Pour boiling water into a heatproof pitcher. Stir in tea and spices; steep 5 minutes. Stir in gelatin and cool. Add juices and sugar; stir until sugar dissolves. Chill and serve over ice. Garnish with orange slices. Refrigerate any leftovers. Makes 3 quarts.

Lynda Robson
Boston, MA

just for fun

Tuck fresh blossoms into vintage soda bottles and line them up on a windowsill. Tint the water in the bottles with a few drops of food coloring.

Citrus Slush

This sweet, sour, icy drink is perfect for a party on a hot day. Tuck any leftover slush back in the freezer and pull out as needed all summer long.

9 c. water
4 c. sugar
12-oz. can frozen lemonade
    concentrate, thawed

12-oz. can frozen orange juice
    concentrate, thawed
2 2-ltr. bottles lemon-lime soda,
    chilled

Bring water and sugar to a boil in a medium saucepan over medium-high heat. Reduce heat; simmer 15 minutes, or until sugar dissolves. Stir in lemonade and orange juice concentrates; cool 30 minutes. Pour into a large container and freeze overnight, or to desired consistency. For each serving, pour about ¾ cup soda and about ½ cup slush into a tall glass. Serves 20 to 25.

Aryn Lentz
Camp Hill, PA

Raspberry Cooler

4 c. raspberries
½ c. sugar
1 c. water, divided

¼ c. orange juice
3-oz. pkg. unflavored gelatin
Garnish: orange peel twists

Combine raspberries, sugar, ¾ cup water and orange juice in a blender; process until smooth and pour into a saucepan. Cook over low heat 5 minutes; remove from heat and cool. Combine gelatin with remaining ¼ cup water, stirring until gelatin dissolves; add to raspberry mixture. Pour into a 4-cup container and freeze 2 hours; the mixture should be soft, not solid. Beat mixture well and freeze until firm. Garnish each serving with an orange peel twist. Serves 4.

Refreshing Citrus Blush

The flavor-filled combination of these succulent fruits will tingle your tongue!

4 ruby red grapefruit, halved　　1 mango, peeled and chopped
3 tangerines, halved　　　　　　1 T. honey

　　Using a juicer, squeeze grapefruit and tangerine halves to yield 4 cups juice; set aside. Place chopped mango and honey in a food processor and process until smooth; add to juice and mix well. Serve chilled. Serves 4 to 6.

make it sparkle

Add club soda, ginger ale or lemon-lime soda to this delicious drink to add a refreshing zip!

Tomato Cocktail

Serve this great appetizer drink for your guests to enjoy while you're putting the finishing touches on brunch.

46-oz. can tomato juice
juice of ½ lemon
1 t. sweet onion, grated

1 t. Worcestershire sauce
⅛ t. hot pepper sauce
Garnish: celery sticks

Combine all ingredients except celery sticks in a large pitcher; stir well and chill. Garnish each serving with a celery stick. Serves 6.

make a garnish buffet

In addition to celery, set out pickled okra, pickled jalapeños, cocktail olives, gherkins, blanched green beans, fresh cucumbers...and even steamed shrimp... for guests to add to their cocktails.

Artichoke-Garlic Dip

Serve this up in a hollowed-out sourdough bread loaf and use chunks of the bread or hearty crackers to dip.

14-oz. can artichokes, drained
   and chopped
½ c. grated Parmesan cheese
8-oz. pkg. cream cheese,
   softened
½ c. mayonnaise

½ t. dill weed
2 cloves garlic, minced
Optional: additional grated
   Parmesan cheese, chopped
   fresh dill

Combine artichokes, ½ cup Parmesan cheese, cream cheese, mayonnaise, dill weed and garlic in an ungreased 10" pie plate. If desired, sprinkle with additional Parmesan cheese. Bake at 400 degrees for 15 minutes, or until golden. Garnish with additional Parmesan cheese and fresh dill, if desired. Makes about 3½ cups.

Carole Larkins
Elmendorf Air Force Base, AK

a little bit lighter...

For a healthier version, swap Neufchâtel cheese for regular cream cheese and and reduced-fat mayonnaise for regular mayonnaise. You'll still get the rich, creamy taste but with less fat and fewer calories!

Easy Mexican Dip

If you prefer a spicier dip, add more taco seasoning mix.

"This simple recipe has been a favorite at the tailgate parties that accompany our biannual community musical. The money raised by the performances goes to our all-volunteer fire department. It's a great cause and a lot of fun!"

—Donna

8-oz. pkg. cream cheese, softened
2 T. taco seasoning mix

¼ c. tomato juice
tortilla chips

Combine cream cheese and taco seasoning mix in a bowl; mix well. Add tomato juice and stir to desired consistency. Serve with tortilla chips. Serves 8 to 10.

Donna Scheletsky
Baden, PA

out of tortilla chips?

Make your own in a flash. Simply slice tortillas into wedges, spray with non-stick vegetable spray and bake at 350 degrees for 5 to 7 minutes.

Spicy Red Salsa

1 tomato, chopped
1 onion, chopped
1 tomatillo, chopped
1 jalapeño pepper, chopped

1 T. fresh cilantro, chopped
1 t. lime juice
¼ t. salt

Combine all ingredients in a small mixing bowl; gently stir to mix. Cover and refrigerate one hour. Store leftovers in the refrigerator for up to one week. Makes 2 cups.

make it milder

For a less spicy version, remove the seeds and membrane from the jalapeño pepper before chopping.

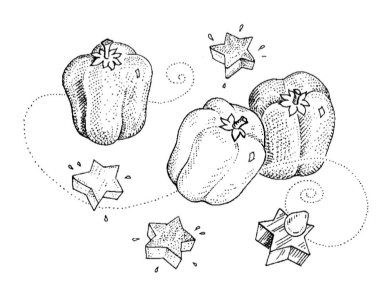

Homemade Guacamole

6 avocados, pitted and peeled
2 to 4 cloves garlic, minced
1 lime, halved and divided
1 tomato, diced
½ onion, diced

salt to taste
Optional: 1 diced jalapeño pepper,
    chopped fresh cilantro
tortilla chips

Combine avocados, garlic and juice of ½ lime in a large bowl; mash to desired consistency. Gently stir in tomato, onion, salt and juice of remaining ½ lime; add jalapeño and cilantro, if using. Cover and chill for 30 minutes to one hour; stir before serving. Serve with tortilla chips. Serves 6 to 8.

Athena Colegrove
Big Spring, TX

keep it green

Be sure to add plenty of lime juice if you are planning on taking this yummy dip to a potluck. The acidity from the lime helps prevent browning. Another trick? Rub oil on plastic wrap and place oiled side directly over the dip when you refrigerate to keep it fresh and bright green.

Slow-Cooker Pub Beer Dip

2 5-oz. jars sharp Cheddar
      cheese spread
8-oz. pkg. cream cheese,
      softened
½ c. regular or non-alcoholic beer
1 t. Worcestershire sauce
5 to 6 drops hot pepper sauce
4 to 5 slices bacon, crisply
      cooked and crumbled
pretzels, crackers or sliced
      vegetables

Combine cheeses, beer and sauces in a greased 2½- to 3-quart slow cooker. Cover and cook on low setting 2 hours, stirring occasionally; the dip will become thicker the longer it cooks. Stir in bacon just before serving, sprinkling some on top. Serve with pretzels, crackers or sliced vegetables. Makes about 4 cups.

Karen Hazelett
Fremont, IN

"We enjoy the time we spend at Lake James in northeast Indiana. Winters at the lake are lonely for year 'rounders, so we started a monthly card club with five other couples. It's a terrific way to see your neighbors during colder months and try each other's recipes. Our friend Jan, who is a wonderful hostess, shared this slow-cooker recipe with us. It was an immediate hit!"

—Karen

Cheesy Fruit and Nut Spread

Try this delicious spread on slices of nut bread too.

8-oz. pkg. cream cheese,
   softened
3 T. honey
1 T. apple brandy or apple juice

¼ c. chopped pecans
½ c. dried apple pieces, chopped
Garnish: chopped pecans
apple and pear slices

Combine cream cheese, honey and brandy or juice in a bowl; mix well. Stir in ¼ cup pecans and dried apple; cover and refrigerate until chilled. Top with additional chopped pecans. Serve with apple and pear slices. Makes about 2 cups.

Lisa Ashton
Aston, PA

give it a twist

Use walnuts or almonds in lieu of pecans. Try dried apricots or cranberries instead of dried apples.

Oniony Crab Dip

Oniony Crab Dip

This dip couldn't be easier to whip up...keep it warm in a slow cooker.

2 8-oz. pkgs. cream cheese,
    softened
3 T. butter
1 bunch green onions, chopped
1 lb. crabmeat

garlic salt to taste
onion salt to taste
crackers and garlic toast
Optional: additional chopped
    green onions

Combine all ingredients except crackers, toast and additional green onions in a microwave-safe bowl; microwave on high until warm. Stir well. Pour into an ungreased slow cooker; cover and keep warm on low setting. Serve with crackers and garlic toast. Garnish with additional green onions, if desired. Serves 24.

Lisa Colombo
Appleton, WI

Creamy Shrimp Spread

4 c. cooked shrimp, peeled
8-oz. pkg. cream cheese, softened
½ c. butter, softened
1 t. salt
½ t. white pepper

1 T. lemon juice
2 t. horseradish sauce
½ t. hot pepper sauce
1 sweet onion, diced

Place shrimp in a food processor and process until smooth; place in a bowl and set aside. Combine cream cheese, butter, salt, white pepper, lemon juice, horseradish sauce and hot pepper sauce in food processor; process until blended. Add to shrimp and mix well; stir in onion. Serves 8.

Dee's Buffalo Dip

2 12.5-oz. cans white chicken, drained and flaked
2 8-oz. pkgs. Neufchâtel cheese, softened
1 c. low-fat ranch salad dressing
¾ c. hot pepper sauce
2 c. shredded reduced-fat Cheddar cheese, divided
Garnish: chopped fresh parsley
assorted vegetables or crackers

Combine chicken and Neufchâtel cheese in a microwave-safe bowl. Microwave, uncovered, on high for 45 seconds; stir well. Add salad dressing, hot pepper sauce and one cup Cheddar cheese; mix well. Spoon into a lightly greased 8"x8" baking pan; sprinkle remaining Cheddar cheese on top. Bake, uncovered, at 350 degrees for 30 to 35 minutes, until hot and bubbly. Garnish with chopped parsley. Serve with assorted vegetables or crackers. Serves 8 to 10.

Deanna Lyons
Roswell, GA

Hot Bacon & Swiss Dip

Always a favorite...this popular flavor combination is unbeatable.

8-oz. pkg. cream cheese, softened
½ c. mayonnaise
1 c. shredded Swiss cheese
2 T. green onions, chopped
8 slices bacon, crisply cooked and crumbled, divided
½ c. round buttery crackers, crushed

Combine cream cheese, mayonnaise, Swiss cheese and green onions; mix well. Add half the bacon; mix well. Spread in an ungreased one-quart casserole dish; top with remaining bacon and crushed crackers. Bake, uncovered, at 350 degrees for 15 minutes. Serve warm. Makes about 3 cups.

Marla Caldwell
Forest, IN

Scrumptious Stuffed Potato Skins

Scrumptious says it all! Plus...this easy-to-make appetizer will satisfy a hungry crowd.

4 baking potatoes, quartered
    lengthwise
olive oil
8-oz. container sour cream
⅓ c. shredded Cheddar cheese
1 t. garlic, minced
1 green onion, chopped

2 t. dried parsley
2 T. bacon bits
½ t. salt
½ t. pepper
Garnish: bacon bits, chopped
    green onions, shredded
    Cheddar cheese

Brush potato skins with olive oil; arrange on an ungreased baking sheet cut-side up. Bake at 400 degrees for 30 minutes; cool. Scoop out insides of potatoes, leaving about ⅛-inch shells; reserve scooped-out potato for another use. Combine remaining ingredients except garnish and spoon into potato skins; return to baking sheet. Bake an additional 20 minutes. Garnish with additional bacon bits, green onions and Cheddar cheese. Makes 16.

Tammy Rowe
Fremont, OH

to top it off...

Serve with sour cream, salsa or anything else you like on your baked potatoes.

Herb-Seasoned Spinach Puffs

Serve with a spicy mustard sauce for dipping.

2 10-oz. pkgs. frozen chopped
   spinach, thawed
2 c. herb-flavored stuffing mix

1 c. grated Parmesan cheese
6 eggs, lightly beaten
⅓ c. butter, softened

Drain and squeeze spinach to remove all liquid; combine with stuffing mix, cheese, eggs and butter and mix well. Form mixture into 2-inch balls and place on a lightly oiled baking sheet. Cover with aluminum foil and refrigerate overnight. Bake at 350 degrees for 15 minutes, or until thoroughly heated; remove from baking sheet and place on paper towels. Serves 8 to 10.

add twinkle

Fill the tiniest terra cotta pots with votive candles to add a warm and cozy glow to your kitchen.

Speedy Sausage Scoops

Keep these four ingredients on hand for a simple appetizer whenever neighbors drop in or for a last-minute party dish.

1 lb. ground pork sausage, browned and drained
8-oz. pkg. cream cheese, softened

10½-oz. pkg. scoop-type corn chips
1 c. shredded Cheddar cheese

Combine sausage and cream cheese in a bowl; mix well. Spoon mixture into corn chip scoops; sprinkle with Cheddar cheese and place on a microwave-safe plate. Microwave on high 30 seconds, or until Cheddar cheese melts. Serve immediately. Serves 6 to 8.

Rebecca Etling
Blairsville, PA

"Crunchy, cheesy, yummy finger food! This is one of my favorite appetizers when I need something fast. If you like your snacks a bit spicier, use hot sausage."

—Rebecca

Pizza Roll Snacks

8-oz. tube refrigerated crescent
    rolls
3 T. pizza sauce
¼ c. grated Parmesan cheese

16 slices pepperoni, divided
⅓ c. shredded mozzarella
    cheese, divided
Garnish: small fresh basil leaves

Unroll crescent roll dough but do not separate; press perforations to seal. Spread pizza sauce evenly over dough, leaving a one-inch border. Sprinkle with Parmesan cheese and roll up, starting with the long side. Using a sharp knife, cut roll-up into 16 slices. Place slices cut-side down on a greased baking sheet. Top each slice with one pepperoni slice and one teaspoon mozzarella cheese. Bake at 375 degrees for 9 to 11 minutes, until edges are golden and cheese melts. Garnish with basil leaves. Makes 16.

Diane Cohen
The Woodlands, TX

"Who needs frozen pizza rolls when it's a snap to make these yummy rolls? My girls love them for after-school snacks. If there are any leftovers, they warm up great in the microwave."

—Diane

Nachos Magnificos

Feeling creative? Vary the ingredients according to your taste!

1 lb. ground beef
1 c. onion, chopped
salt and pepper to taste
2 15-oz. cans refried beans
4-oz. can green chiles, chopped
1 to 2 c. salsa
1 c. shredded Cheddar cheese
1 c. shredded mozzarella cheese

1 c. shredded Monterey Jack
  cheese
6-oz. container guacamole
2¼-oz. can black olives, drained
  and sliced
1 c. green onions, chopped
1½ c. sour cream
tortilla chips

Brown beef and onion in a skillet; drain and season with salt and pepper. Lightly grease a 13"x9" baking pan; spread refried beans on bottom and add beef mixture. Layer on chiles and salsa. Sprinkle with cheeses; cover and bake at 400 degrees for 35 to 40 minutes. Top with guacamole, olives, green onions and sour cream. Serve immediately with tortilla chips. Serves 10 to 12.

South Street Tortilla Roll-Ups

A wonderful appetizer that's sure to please!

8-oz. pkg. cream cheese,
    softened
1 onion, chopped
8-oz. container sour cream
1¼-oz. pkg. taco seasoning mix
8-oz. pkg shredded Cheddar
    cheese

4½-oz. can chopped green chiles
2 tomatoes, chopped
hot pepper sauce to taste
10 flour tortillas
Garnish: salsa, guacamole

Combine cream cheese, onion, sour cream and taco seasoning mix in a large bowl; mix until smooth. Fold in Cheddar cheese, chiles, tomatoes and hot pepper sauce, blending well. Spread mixture on tortillas; roll up tortillas and refrigerate until cream cheese mixture is firm. Slice roll-ups and serve cold with salsa and guacamole. Serves 8 to 10.

spice it up!

Keep spicy salsa and a bottle of hot sauce on the table for guests who want a little more kick.

Glazed Cocktail Sausages

Put these savory sausages in your slow cooker the morning of the big football game...they'll be ready by kickoff!

2 16-oz. pkgs. mini smoked
    sausages
1 c. apricot preserves
½ c. maple syrup
2 T. bourbon or 1 to 2 t. vanilla
    extract

Combine all ingredients in an ungreased slow cooker. Cover and cook on low setting for 4 hours. Serves 16 to 20.

Janice Dorsey
San Antonio, TX

Nana's Slow-Cooker Meatballs

"These meatballs have been famous in my family for generations and are begged for at parties by young and old alike. Use a slow cooker to finish the cooking and keep them warm."

—Stephanie

2½ c. catsup
1 c. brown sugar, packed
2 T. Worcestershire sauce

2 lbs. ground beef
1.35-oz. pkg. onion soup mix
5-oz. can evaporated milk

Combine catsup, brown sugar and Worcestershire sauce in a slow cooker; stir well and cover. Turn slow cooker to high setting and allow mixture to warm while preparing the meatballs. Combine beef, onion soup mix and evaporated milk; mix well and form into one-inch balls. Place meatballs on an ungreased 15"x10" jelly-roll pan. Bake at 325 degrees for 20 minutes; drain. Spoon meatballs into slow cooker and reduce setting to low. Cover and cook 2 to 3 hours, stirring gently after one hour. Makes 4 dozen.

Stephanie Norton
Saginaw, TX

pick the perfect pot

Choose the right size slow cooker for the job. To ensure safe food and even cooking, you'll need one that is one-half to two-thirds full when all the meatballs are added.

Easy Cheesy Manicotti,
page 46

memorable main dishes

From meat-free manicotti to meaty pork chops, these hearty family favorites anchor any spread…be it a fancy buffet or a cozy weeknight dinner. Spice it up with Chili-Rubbed Steaks (page 74). Try Cornmeal Fried Catfish & Fresh Tartar Sauce (page 48) for a quick summer supper and Louisiana Shrimp Boil (page 54) for a fun outdoor feast. Buttermilk Fried Chicken (page 61) is a picnic must and Slow-Cooker Farmhouse Pot Roast (page 78) cooks to perfection with minimal attention.

Easy Cheesy Manicotti

(pictured on page 44)

12-oz. pkg. manicotti, uncooked
1½ t. salt, divided
1 T. olive oil
8-oz. pkg. cream cheese, softened
2 c. cottage cheese
12-oz. pkg. shredded Monterey
    Jack cheese

1 egg, beaten
1 T. fresh parsley, chopped
1 clove garlic, minced
12-oz. pkg. shredded mozzarella
    cheese, divided
24-oz. jar spaghetti sauce
Optional: chopped fresh parsley

Cook manicotti according to package directions, using one teaspoon salt and one tablespoon oil; drain and set aside. Combine cheeses, egg, parsley, garlic, remaining ½ teaspoon salt, and two-thirds of the mozzarella cheese in a large bowl; set aside. Spread a thin layer of spaghetti sauce on the bottom of an ungreased 13"x9" baking pan. Spoon cheese filling into each manicotti, filling ¾ full; arrange on top of sauce. Pour remaining sauce over manicotti; bake, uncovered, at 350 degrees for 30 to 45 minutes. Top with remaining mozzarella 10 minutes before done. Cool 10 minutes before serving. Garnish with additional parsley, if desired. Serves 6.

Robin Argyle
Kalkaska, MI

for new parents

Make this for a new neighbor or a friend who just had a baby. Assemble it in a casserole dish they can keep and cover with foil. Deliver with baking directions, a serving spoon, a salad and a loaf of bread so all they have to do is heat and serve.

Salmon with Lemon-Parsley Sauce

Treat your family and guests with this easy-to-make dish.

8 4-oz. salmon fillets
⅓ c. mayonnaise
2 T. sweet onion, diced

1 T. fresh parsley, chopped
2 t. lemon juice

Place fillets in a lightly oiled 13"x9" baking pan. Combine remaining ingredients in a small bowl, stirring until smooth; spread evenly over fillets. Bake at 425 degrees for 15 minutes. Serves 8.

the dish on baking dishes...

Shopping for a new casserole dish? Consider a deep 13"x9" glass baking pan. It retains heat well, helps create crisp golden edges and can be used for everything from main dishes to delicious desserts. Plus, most are dishwasher safe!

Cornmeal Fried Catfish & Fresh Tartar Sauce

Serve these easy-to-prepare fillets with homemade tartar sauce or your favorite bottled cocktail sauce and hot sauce.

3 large or 6 small catfish fillets	½ t. pepper
½ c. mustard	2 T. oil
1 c. cornmeal	lemon wedges
1 t. salt	

Rinse and dry fillets; brush with mustard. Combine cornmeal, salt and pepper in a large plastic zipping bag; shake bag to mix well. Pour oil into a skillet and place over medium-high heat. Add one fillet to bag and shake to coat; add fillet to skillet, fry until golden on both sides and place in a brown paper bag to keep crisp. Repeat with remaining fillets, adding more oil, if needed. Serve with lemon wedges and Fresh Tartar Sauce. Serves 6.

Fresh Tartar Sauce:

½ c. sour cream	2 T. onion, diced
½ c. mayonnaise	1 T. fresh parsley, chopped
1 t. lemon juice	

Combine all ingredients in a small bowl and mix well. Cover and refrigerate until chilled. Makes 1¼ cups.

Chive & Dijon Crab Cakes

These tasty crab cakes are crunchy outside yet moist inside.

1 lb. fresh crabmeat, flaked
½ c. soft bread crumbs
2 T. fresh parsley, chopped
2 T. whipping cream
1 T. lemon juice
2 t. fresh chives, chopped

1 t. Dijon mustard
⅛ t. cayenne pepper
1 egg
1 egg yolk
⅓ c. dry bread crumbs
½ c. butter

Combine crabmeat, soft bread crumbs, parsley, cream, lemon juice, chives, mustard, cayenne pepper, egg and egg yolk in a large bowl; stir well. Shape mixture into 8 patties; set aside. Place dry bread crumbs in a bowl; dip each patty in bread crumbs, covering both sides well. Melt butter in a large skillet over medium-high heat. Add crab cakes and cook 5 minutes, or until golden on both sides, turning once. Repeat with remaining crab cakes. Serves 4.

make 'em minis!

Turn this dish into an elegant appetizer. Shape mixture into bite-size patties and cook until golden. Serve with a dollop of crème fraîche and chopped fresh chives.

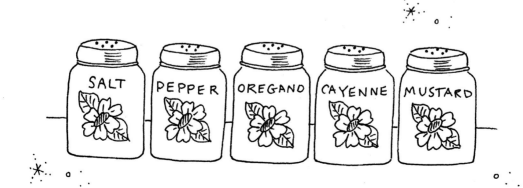

Donna's Shrimp Scampi Dinner

½ c. butter
2 t. Worcestershire sauce
¼ c. cooking sherry or chicken broth
1 to 2 t. garlic, minced
1 T. sugar
2 T. lemon juice

1 to 1½ lbs. uncooked medium shrimp, peeled and cleaned
¼ c. fresh parsley, minced
3 c. cooked rice
Garnish: grated Parmesan cheese

"This recipe is always a hit with my family & friends! Add Roasted Asparagus and Creamy Peach Whirl to make it a meal."

—Donna

Melt butter in a saucepan over low heat. Stir in Worcestershire sauce, sherry or broth, garlic, sugar and lemon juice; mix well and remove from heat. Arrange shrimp in a single layer in a lightly greased 11"x7" baking pan. Spoon butter mixture over shrimp; sprinkle with parsley. Broil at medium heat 5 minutes, or until shrimp turn pink. Spoon over cooked rice; sprinkle with Parmesan cheese. Serves 4.

Roasted Asparagus:

Toss one pound asparagus with one tablespoon olive oil; arrange on an ungreased baking sheet. Sprinkle with salt to taste. Bake at 400 degrees for 8 to 10 minutes, until tender. Serves 4.

Creamy Peach Whirl:

Combine 2 cups sliced peaches, 2 cups vanilla ice cream, one cup milk and 2 tablespoons powdered sugar in a blender; process until smooth. Sprinkle with nutmeg. Serves 4.

Donna Eichner
Whitehall, PA

Shrimp Kabobs

Ready to eat in minutes!

3 carrots, cut diagonally
1 green pepper, cut into 1-inch
    strips
¼ c. water
½ t. orange zest

½ c. orange juice
2 t. fresh thyme, minced
2 t. canola oil
12 to 16 uncooked large shrimp,
    peeled and cleaned

Combine carrots, green pepper and water in a saucepan. Bring to a boil, cover and simmer 3 minutes. In a small bowl, combine orange zest, orange juice, thyme and oil. Set aside. Lightly grease grill or broiler pan. Thread shrimp, carrots and peppers on skewers; place on grill. Baste kabobs with orange juice mixture and grill 3 inches from heat for 2 minutes. Turn kabobs, baste and grill another 3 minutes, or until shrimp turn pink. Serves 4.

Louisiana Shrimp Boil

Just for fun, serve this meal with sliced French bread outdoors on a picnic table…and be sure to pass plenty of paper towels!

2 onions, sliced
2 lemons, sliced
3-oz. pkg. crab boil seasoning
Optional: hot pepper sauce
    to taste

16 new redskin potatoes
4 ears corn, husked and halved
2 lbs. uncooked medium shrimp
    in the shell

Fill a very large stockpot half full with water; add onions, lemons, seasoning and hot pepper sauce, if using. Bring water to a boil over medium-high heat; add potatoes and boil 10 minutes. Add corn; boil 5 minutes. Add shrimp; boil until shrimp turn pink and float to the surface. Drain; serve on a large platter. Serves 4.

Janet Bowlin
Fayetteville, AR

Slow-Cooker Chicken & Dumplings

With a slow cooker, you can serve your family a homestyle dinner even after a busy day away from home.

1½ lbs. boneless, skinless chicken
    breasts, cubed
2 potatoes, cubed
2 c. baby carrots
2 stalks celery, sliced
2 10¾-oz. cans cream of
    chicken soup

1 c. water
1 t. dried thyme
¼ t. pepper
2 c. biscuit baking mix
⅔ c. milk

Place chicken, potatoes, carrots and celery in a slow cooker; set aside. In a medium bowl, combine soup, water, thyme and pepper; pour over chicken mixture. Cover and cook on low setting 7 to 8 hours, until juices run clear when chicken is pierced. Mix together baking mix and milk; drop into slow cooker by large spoonfuls. Tilt lid to vent and cook on high setting 30 minutes, or until dumplings are cooked in center. Serves 8.

Rhonda Reeder
Ellicott City, MD

cook slow & go!

Slow cookers are perfect for potlucks. Many come with lids that lock into place. Plus, cookers keep food warm, making them ideal for the buffet line.

Easy Garlic-Parmesan Chicken

¾ c. mayonnaise
½ c. grated Parmesan cheese
1 t. garlic powder
1 t. Italian seasoning

4 to 6 boneless, skinless chicken breasts
1 c. Italian-flavored dry bread crumbs

Mix mayonnaise, cheese and seasonings in a shallow bowl. Coat chicken breasts with mixture; cover with bread crumbs. Arrange in a lightly greased 13"x9" baking pan. Bake, uncovered, at 425 degrees for 20 to 25 minutes, until golden and juices run clear when chicken is pierced. Serves 4 to 6.

Denise Allison
Gig Harbor, WA

"My handy tip...for easy clean-up, line the pan with aluminum foil before spraying it with non-stick vegetable spray."

—Denise

Chicken Oregano

Serve over thin spaghetti...pass the Parmesan cheese, please!

1½ lbs. boneless, skinless chicken breasts
15-oz. can tomato sauce
28-oz. can diced tomatoes
1 green pepper, thinly sliced

1 onion, thinly sliced
1 t. garlic salt
1 t. dried oregano
salt and pepper to taste
½ c. shredded mozzarella cheese

Place chicken in a lightly greased 13"x9" baking pan. Top with sauce and tomatoes. Arrange green pepper and onion on top; sprinkle with seasonings and cheese. Bake, uncovered, at 375 degrees for 30 minutes, or until juices run clear when chicken is pierced. Serves 4.

Julie Bruninga
Edwardsville, IL

Honey Chicken Stir-Fry

Measure out the seasonings before you begin to stir-fry…you'll find this dish comes together very quickly.

2 lbs. boneless, skinless chicken
    strips
¼ c. honey, divided
1 egg, beaten
⅓ c. plus 1 T. water, divided
1 t. Worcestershire sauce
½ t. dried thyme
¼ t. lemon-pepper seasoning
¼ t. garlic powder
⅛ t. dried oregano
⅛ t. dried marjoram
2 T. vegetable oil
1 T. cornstarch
14-oz. pkg. frozen stir-fry
    vegetables
¼ t. salt
cooked rice

Combine chicken, 2 tablespoons honey, egg, ⅓ cup water, Worcestershire sauce and seasonings; set aside. Heat oil in a wok or large skillet over medium-high heat. Add chicken a few pieces at a time; cook and stir until golden. Remove chicken from wok; keep warm. Mix cornstarch with remaining 2 tablespoons honey and one tablespoon water; set aside. Add vegetables to wok; sprinkle with salt. Cook over medium heat until vegetables begin to thaw; drizzle with cornstarch mixture. Continue cooking until vegetables are tender; stir in chicken and heat through. Serve with rice. Serves 4 to 6.

Lynn Ruble
Decatur, IN

Buttermilk Fried Chicken

1 c. buttermilk	½ t. pepper
3½ lbs. chicken, cut up	vegetable oil
1 c. plus 3 T. all-purpose flour, divided	1 c. milk
	1½ c. water
1½ t. salt	salt and pepper to taste

Pour buttermilk over chicken pieces in a large shallow dish; cover and refrigerate one hour. Combine one cup flour, salt and pepper in a large plastic zipping bag. Drain chicken and add to bag, one piece at a time, shaking to coat. Place on wax paper; let stand 15 minutes. Heat ¼ inch oil in a large cast-iron skillet over medium heat. Add chicken; cook until golden on all sides. Reduce heat to low; cover and simmer 25 to 30 minutes, until juices run clear when chicken is pierced. Uncover; cook, turning often, an additional 5 minutes. Drain chicken on paper towels; keep warm. For gravy, pour off all except ¼ cup drippings from skillet. Stir in remaining 3 tablespoons flour over low heat until well blended; gradually add milk. Slowly stir in water; bring to a boil over medium heat. Cook 2 minutes, or until thickened, stirring constantly. Add salt and pepper to taste. Serve gravy with chicken. Serves 6.

Nancy Wise
Little Rock, AR

"This is pure, down-home goodness...delicious warm from the skillet or wrapped in wax paper to savor cold as a picnic lunch with coleslaw."

—Nancy

be careful with cast iron

Don't use soap, abrasive chemicals or rough sponges to clean your cast-iron skillet. Wash it by hand with hot water and a sponge. Remove crusty residue by scrubbing the pan with kosher salt, then rinse with water. Pat dry and heat on the stove over low heat until all moisture is removed.

Skillet Chicken & Mushrooms

1½ lbs. boneless, skinless
    chicken breasts
salt and pepper to taste
3 T. butter, divided
1 yellow onion, chopped

1 lb. sliced mushrooms
¼ c. Madeira wine or chicken
    broth
1 T. Worcestershire sauce
1 T. fresh tarragon, chopped

Sprinkle chicken generously with salt and pepper. In a large skillet over medium-high heat, melt 2 tablespoons butter. Cook chicken 8 minutes, or until golden on both sides. Transfer chicken to a plate. Melt remaining one tablespoon butter in skillet over medium heat. Add onion; sauté just until softened, about 3 minutes. Add mushrooms; sauté until juices are released, about 5 minutes. Stir in wine or broth and Worcestershire sauce. Return chicken and any juices from the plate to the pan. Spoon mushroom mixture over chicken. Reduce heat to medium-low; cover and cook 20 minutes, or until juices run clear when chicken is pierced. Stir in tarragon and additional salt and pepper, as desired. Serves 4.

Tina Wright
Atlanta, GA

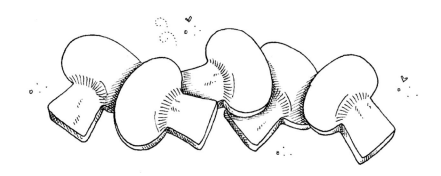

Spinach & Cheese-Stuffed Chicken Breasts

Try serving this dish over wild rice.

6 5-oz. boneless, skinless chicken breasts	14-oz. pkg. frozen chopped spinach, thawed and drained well
¼ c. vegetable oil	½ c. cottage cheese
2 T. dried thyme	¼ c. grated Parmesan cheese
2 T. butter	½ t. dried basil
¼ c. sweet onion, diced	

Brush chicken breasts with oil, sprinkle with thyme and set aside. Melt butter in a saucepan and sauté onion until tender. Remove from heat and set aside. Combine spinach with cottage cheese, Parmesan cheese and basil in a large mixing bowl. Stir in sautéed onions and mix well. Place a portion of the stuffing mixture in center of each chicken breast and bring sides to center, overlapping. Secure with metal skewers and place in a lightly greased 13"x9" baking pan. Bake at 375 degrees for 30 minutes, or until juices run clear when chicken is pierced. Remove skewers before serving. Serves 6.

Mushroom-Garlic-Chicken Pizza

12-inch Italian pizza crust
¾ c. ranch salad dressing
2 T. garlic, minced
1 chicken breast, cooked and
　　sliced
2　4-oz. cans sliced mushrooms,
　　drained
salt and pepper to taste
8-oz. pkg. shredded mozzarella
　　cheese
Optional: fresh oregano leaves,
　　red pepper flakes

"This recipe gets a big 'YUM' at our house...try it! It's a great way to use leftover baked or grilled chicken too."

—Judy

Place crust on an ungreased pizza pan or baking sheet. Spread salad dressing and garlic on crust. Arrange sliced chicken and mushrooms on top. Add salt and pepper to taste; cover with cheese. Bake at 400 degrees for 8 to 10 minutes, until cheese melts. Cut into wedges. Garnish with oregano and red pepper, if desired. Serves 6 to 8.

Judy Davis
Muskogee, OK

make it a pizza party!

Provide crusts, sauces and toppings and let your guests create individual pies. Be sure to include a variety of meats, cheeses and veggies. Serve alongside a freshly tossed salad for a balanced dinner.

Chicken Turnovers

"This is one of the most-requested recipes in our family of five hungry boys...a 13-year-old and four 10-year-olds (yes, quadruplets!). It is definitely comfort food and we hope everyone who tries it will enjoy it! I double this recipe to feed my hungry crew."

—Angela

4 c. cooked chicken, cubed
8-oz. pkg. cream cheese, softened
½ c. milk
1 T. onion, minced
1 t. salt
⅛ t. pepper
2 8-oz. tubes refrigerated
    crescent rolls

1 T. margarine, melted
¾ c. grated Parmesan cheese
2 10¾-oz. cans cream of
    chicken soup
⅔ c. milk

Blend chicken, cream cheese, milk, onion, salt and pepper; set aside. Separate each tube of crescent rolls into 4 rectangles; press to seal perforations. Spoon ½ cup chicken mixture into center of each rectangle; pull up corners to form a triangle and press to seal. Place turnovers on an ungreased baking sheet. Brush tops with margarine; sprinkle with Parmesan cheese. Bake, uncovered, at 350 degrees for 20 to 25 minutes, until golden. While turnovers are baking, combine soup and milk in a saucepan; heat until bubbly. Spoon soup mixture over turnovers. Serves 4 to 6.

Angela Bettencourt
Mukilteo, WA

Potato & Ham Frittata

2 c. frozen hashbrowns with
   onions and peppers
3 T. butter
6 eggs

2 T. water
pepper to taste
1 c. cooked ham, diced

"We love this quick & easy recipe for breakfast, lunch or dinner."

—Eve

Cook hashbrowns in butter in a skillet over medium heat until golden, stirring occasionally. Whisk together eggs, water and pepper; stir in ham. Pour over hashbrowns in skillet. Cook over low heat 9 to 10 minutes. As eggs set, run a spatula around edge of skillet, lifting edges to allow uncooked portion to flow underneath. Continue cooking and lifting edges until eggs are almost set. Remove from heat. Cover; let stand 3 to 4 minutes before cutting into wedges. Serves 4.

Eve Welch
Accokeek, MD

Apricot-Glazed Pork Chops

⅓ c. apricot preserves
⅓ c. white wine or apple juice
½ t. ground ginger

2 T. vegetable oil
4 pork chops
salt and pepper to taste

Mix preserves, wine or juice and ginger in a small bowl; set aside. Heat oil in a large skillet over medium-high heat. Add pork chops; sprinkle with salt and pepper. Cook 4 minutes on each side, or until golden. Remove pork chops from skillet; keep warm. Turn down heat to medium-low. Add preserves mixture to skillet and simmer 4 minutes, or until thickened. Return pork chops to skillet. Cook about one minute on each side, or until well coated with sauce. Serves 4.

Cindy Snavely

keep the glaze, swap the meat

Love the rich flavor of this glaze? Try brushing it on grilled chicken or baked salmon.

Barbecued Baby Back Ribs

Boiling the ribs first tenderizes them and removes excess fat. Serve with white bread and iced tea.

2 T. olive oil
1 onion, chopped
1 stalk celery
1 clove garlic, minced
1 c. catsup

¼ c. brown sugar, packed
¼ c. red wine vinegar
2 T. Worcestershire sauce
1 T. Dijon mustard
3 lbs. baby back ribs

Heat oil in a saucepan over medium-high heat; add onion, celery and garlic. Sauté about 5 minutes, or until tender. Add all remaining ingredients except ribs; stir and simmer about 10 minutes. Place sauce in a food processor and process until smooth. Allow sauce to cool slightly. Bring a large stockpot of water to a boil; simmer ribs, covered, about 20 minutes. Drain ribs and dry with paper towels; baste generously with sauce. Grill over high heat 5 to 6 minutes on one side. Turn ribs and baste again. Grill 6 minutes longer. Serves 4.

garden on the move

Recycle an old wagon into a movable garden filled with pots of herbs, flowers, lettuce or carrots...how clever!

Rosemary Pork Loin

2 T. butter
2 1-lb. pork tenderloins
salt and pepper to taste
2 c. sliced mushrooms
¼ c. onion, finely chopped

3 T. fresh rosemary, chopped
2 cloves garlic, minced
2 T. cooking sherry or apple
    juice
Garnish: fresh rosemary sprigs

Melt butter in a heavy skillet over medium-high heat. Sprinkle pork tenderloins with salt and pepper to taste. Brown pork quickly in butter, about one minute on each side. Remove pork to an ungreased roasting pan, reserving drippings in skillet, and bake pork at 350 degrees for 20 to 25 minutes, until a thermometer registers 145 degrees. Let stand 5 minutes before slicing and placing on a platter. Add remaining ingredients (except sherry or juice and garnish) to skillet. Cook and stir over low heat several minutes, or until mushrooms and onion are almost tender. Stir in sherry or juice. Spoon mushroom mixture over pork slices. Garnish with rosemary. Serves 8.

Carrie O'Shea
Marina Del Rey, CA

"I grow rosemary in my garden, so I'm always looking for recipes to use it in. I've tried many chicken dishes, but I had never paired pork and rosemary until my sister shared this recipe with me. Yum!"

—Carrie

company's coming!

Whip up some creamy mashed potatoes and crisp green beans to turn this into a sophisticated supper. Add any extra rosemary sprigs to the centerpiece for a pleasing aroma.

Chili-Rubbed Steaks

Rubs are a great, quick way to give steaks delicious flavor.

1 T. ground cumin
2 t. chili powder
½ t. salt

⅛ t. pepper
3 boneless sirloin steaks, about
    ½-inch thick

Mix together seasonings and rub on both sides of steaks; let stand 5 to 10 minutes. Lightly oil grill rack. Grill steaks over medium heat 3 to 5 minutes per side for medium-rare. Slice each steak in half; mound each with a generous portion of Chunky Guacamole Salsa. Serve any remaining guacamole on the side. Serves 6.

Chunky Guacamole Salsa:

Place 2 peeled and diced avocados in a medium bowl. Add 2 chopped plum tomatoes and one chopped jalapeño pepper; set aside. Mix together 2 tablespoons each lime juice, chopped shallots and chopped fresh cilantro in a small bowl. Add 1½ teaspoons ground cumin and ½ teaspoon salt; whisk in 2 tablespoons vegetable oil. Pour over avocado mixture; mix well. Serves 6.

Beverly Ray
Brandon, FL

Teriyaki Steak

Leave in marinade overnight for extra-flavorful steak.

¾ c. teriyaki sauce
1 T. fresh ginger, peeled
    and finely chopped

2 T. dry sherry or soy sauce
1 lb. well-trimmed beef top
    round steak, cut into cubes

Combine teriyaki sauce, ginger and sherry in a small bowl. Pour mixture over steak cubes and marinate in refrigerator 6 to 8 hours, turning occasionally. Remove steak from marinade; discard marinade. Place steak cubes on skewers and grill 5 minutes on each side over high heat, or until desired doneness. Serves 2 to 4.

for easy clean-up

Make the marinade in a 2-gallon plastic zipping bag, sealing tightly and shaking to combine. Place steak cubes in bag and seal again. Put bag in a casserole dish and refrigerate to marinate overnight. After skewering the steak cubes, discard the bag!

Peppered Beef in Parsley Crust

Serve thinly sliced with horseradish sauce on the side.

2 T. whole peppercorns
¼ c. butter, softened

1 c. fresh parsley, chopped
2-lb. beef tenderloin roast

Grind peppercorns until coarse and spread evenly on a large platter. In a small mixing bowl, blend together butter and parsley. Spread butter mixture over roast, covering all sides evenly. Place roast on platter and roll in cracked peppercorns until evenly coated. Transfer roast to a lightly greased roasting pan. Bake at 425 degrees for one hour, or until meat thermometer registers 135 degrees; this will produce a rare roast. Let stand 5 to 10 minutes before slicing. Serves 6 to 8.

save the leftovers!

Serve any remaining beef on sliced bread with horseradish for an easy and tasty lunch the next day.

Slow-Cooker Farmhouse Pot Roast

This roast is fall-apart tender and makes its own gravy.

3-lb. beef chuck roast
salt and pepper to taste
8-oz. pkg. whole mushrooms
16 new redskin potatoes
½ lb. carrots, sliced
3 stalks celery, chopped

14½-oz. can beef broth
2 c. water
26-oz. can cream of mushroom
   soup
Optional: chopped fresh parsley

Season roast with salt and pepper and brown on all sides in a skillet over high heat. Place roast in an ungreased slow cooker; top with vegetables. In a medium bowl, blend together broth, water and soup; pour over roast. Cover and cook on low setting 6 to 8 hours, until roast is very tender. Garnish with parsley, if desired. Serves 6.

Cherylann Smith
Elfland, NC

Grilled Garlic Burgers

Serve these with a platter of toppings…fresh romaine lettuce and slices of vine-ripened tomato, cheese, pickles and onion…and let picky eaters top their own.

1¾ lbs. lean ground beef
2 T. garlic, minced
½ c. onion, finely chopped
2 t. salt
2 t. pepper, freshly ground
6 oz. fresh horseradish, peeled
    and shredded

1 T. vegetable oil
2 T. mustard
½ c. plus 2 T. catsup
2 T. sour cream
4 fresh onion buns, split
    and grilled

Mix beef, garlic, onion, salt and pepper in a mixing bowl. Shape into 4 patties. Sprinkle with horseradish and press into meat. Coat a grill rack or large skillet with oil and cook burgers over medium-high heat 4 to 5 minutes per side. While cooking, mix together mustard, catsup and sour cream. Top burgers with catsup mixture and serve on grilled buns. Serves 4.

Macaroni & Corn Bake, page 84

cozy casseroles & one-dish wonders

Who doesn't love the comfort of a casserole or the ease of a dish that dirties only one pot? The simple but hearty recipes in this chapter are great for gatherings any time of day. Choose Cheesy Ham Strata (page 109) for breakfast or brunch, Southwestern Casserole (page 115) for game night and Old-Fashioned Chicken Pot Pie (page 96) for a Sunday supper. Guests are sure to love the Creamy Turkey Lasagna (page 103)...it's one of our favorites.

Macaroni & Corn Bake

(pictured on page 82)

14¾-oz. can creamed corn
15¼-oz. can corn
1 c. elbow macaroni, uncooked
¼ c. butter, softened

1 c. pasteurized process cheese
    spread, cubed
pepper to taste

Combine all ingredients in a large bowl and mix well; spoon into a lightly greased 2-quart casserole dish. Bake, uncovered, at 350 degrees for 45 minutes. Serves 6 to 8.

Jennifer Steenblock
Des Moines, IA

Macaroni & Cheese

Creamy and rich, this dish guarantees smiles around the table.

16-oz. pkg. elbow macaroni,
   cooked and kept warm
½ c. margarine
2 12-oz. cans evaporated milk
salt to taste
16-oz. jar double Cheddar sauce
16-oz. pkg. mild Cheddar
   cheese, cubed

Combine warm macaroni and margarine in a large bowl. Stir until margarine melts; stir in milk, salt and cheese sauce. Spoon mixture into a lightly greased 13"x9" baking pan; add cheese cubes and mix. Bake, uncovered, at 350 degrees for 45 minutes, or until bubbly and golden. Serves 12.

Connie Cook
Farmville, VA

down-home comfort...

Invite friends over for a casual mac-and-cheese dinner and ask them to bring other side dishes. You'll have a complete meal and great company!

Cheesy Spinach Pie

Two cheeses combine to make this dish delectable.

2 c. cottage cheese
⅔ c. feta cheese, crumbled
¼ t. pepper
10-oz. pkg. frozen chopped
    spinach, thawed and drained

3 eggs
¼ c. butter, melted
2 T. all-purpose flour
2 t. dried, minced onion

Combine ingredients in order listed; mix well. Spread into a greased 1½-quart casserole dish. Bake, uncovered, at 350 degrees for 45 minutes, or until center is set. Serves 8.

Janine Kuras
Warren, MI

beef it up

To make this dish a hearty main course, add cooked meats such as deli roast chicken, roasted turkey or spicy sausage crumbles.

Creamy Spinach Ravioli

To make this tasty dish in a snap, use ravioli and spinach in boil-in-the-bag packages. Add halved cherry tomatoes for extra color and flavor.

25-oz. pkg. frozen cheese ravioli
2 9-oz. pkgs. frozen creamed
    spinach

salt and pepper to taste
Garnish: shaved Parmesan
    cheese

Prepare ravioli and spinach separately, according to package directions; drain. Place ravioli in a large serving bowl; top with creamed spinach and toss to coat. Add salt and pepper to taste; garnish with Parmesan cheese. Serves 4.

Kimberly Pierotti
Milmay, NJ

ravioli night...

Weekly theme nights make meal planning simple.
Have family members choose their favorites.
They'll look forward to Spaghetti Monday and
Tex-Mex Tuesday...and you'll always know the
answer to "What's for dinner?"

Chiles Rellenos Casserole

We love chiles rellenos, but stuffing the individual chiles is a lot of fuss. This yummy recipe comes together in a jiffy!

2 8-oz. cans whole green chiles, drained
1 lb. Monterey Jack cheese, sliced
6 eggs, beaten
1½ c. all-purpose flour
2 c. milk
3 T. shortening, melted and slightly cooled
¼ t. salt

Layer chiles and cheese slices in a greased 13"x9" baking pan; set aside. Combine eggs, flour, milk, shortening and salt in a bowl; whisk well and pour over cheese. Bake, uncovered, at 350 degrees for 30 minutes, or until bubbly and golden. Serves 6 to 8.

Chanelle Rey
Ordway, CO

over the top

Serve this casserole with an assortment of toppings. Homemade guacamole, spicy salsa and sour cream are some of our favorites.

One-Dish Tuna & Noodles

This is one of those simple dishes we all remember from childhood.

10¾-oz. can cream of
    mushroom soup
⅔ c. water
2 t. chopped pimento

4 oz. American cheese, sliced
7-oz. can tuna, drained
4 oz. egg noodles, cooked

Combine soup and ⅔ cup water in a medium saucepan and place over medium heat; cook until smooth, stirring frequently. Fold in pimento and cheese; stir until cheese melts. Remove from heat and set aside. Combine tuna and noodles in a bowl and mix well; spoon into a lightly greased shallow 2-quart casserole dish. Pour cheese mixture on top; stir gently to mix. Bake, uncovered, at 375 degrees for 30 minutes. Serves 6.

Tina Wright
Atlanta, GA

remember the label

When freezing casseroles, be sure to label them with the date, recipe name and reheating instructions. This ensures safe food and easy go-to meals.

Savory Lowcountry Shrimp & Grits

Paired with a fresh spinach salad, this is a favorite meal...and using a slow cooker makes it easy to prepare, even on a busy day.

6 c. chicken broth
¾ t. salt
1½ c. quick-cooking grits, uncooked
1 green pepper, chopped
½ c. red pepper, chopped
6 green onions, chopped
2 cloves garlic, chopped
1½ lbs. uncooked small shrimp, peeled and cleaned

2 T. butter
1½ c. shredded sharp Cheddar cheese
1½ c. shredded Monterey Jack cheese
2 10-oz. cans diced tomatoes with green chiles, drained
Optional: ¼ t. cayenne pepper, chopped green onions, chopped fresh parsley

Place broth, salt and grits in an ungreased slow cooker; cover and cook on low setting 6 to 8 hours. Two hours before serving, sauté peppers, onions, garlic and shrimp in butter in a skillet over medium-high heat about 5 minutes, or until vegetables are tender and shrimp are pink. Add vegetable mixture, cheeses, tomatoes and cayenne pepper, if using, to slow cooker. Turn to high setting; cover and cook an additional 2 hours. Garnish with green onions and parsley, if desired. Serves 4 to 6.

Sharon Candler
Villa Rica, GA

Chicken Enchilada Casserole

1 onion, chopped
½ c. margarine
10¾-oz. can cream of chicken soup
10¾-oz. can cream of mushroom soup
4½-oz. can chopped green chiles

1 c. chicken broth
6 to 8 flour tortillas, torn into bite-size pieces and divided
4 boneless, skinless chicken breasts, cubed
½ lb. Cheddar cheese, sliced

Sauté onion in margarine in a large skillet over medium heat until tender; add soups, green chiles and broth, mixing well. Layer half the tortilla pieces in a lightly greased 13"x9" baking pan. Layer chicken, cheese slices and remaining tortilla pieces on top; add soup mixture. Bake, uncovered, at 350 degrees for 30 minutes, or until heated through. Serves 6.

Chrissy Boyd
Collinsville, OK

twice as nice

This recipe doubles easily. Make one to enjoy tonight and save the other to share with friends and family.

Chicken and Rice Casserole

So easy and versatile...and it's even better the next day.

4 to 5 boneless, skinless chicken
    breasts, cooked and cubed
13½-oz. can French-style green
    beans
1 c. mayonnaise
8-oz. can sliced water chestnuts

10¾-oz. can cream of celery
    soup
6.9-oz. pkg. chicken-flavored
    rice vermicelli mix, cooked
salt and pepper to taste
Garnish: grated Parmesan cheese

Combine all ingredients except Parmesan cheese in a large bowl and mix well. Spoon into a lightly greased 13"x9" baking pan. Bake, uncovered, at 350 degrees for 30 to 45 minutes, until golden. Sprinkle with Parmesan cheese. Serves 8.

Julia Humphreys
Cleveland, TN

Old-Fashioned Chicken Pot Pie

This makes two savory pies...share one with a neighbor or freeze it to use later.

4 9-inch frozen pie crusts, thawed and divided
5 to 6 boneless, skinless chicken breasts, cooked and chopped
1 onion, chopped
10¾-oz. can cream of chicken soup
10¾-oz. can cream of mushroom soup
8-oz. container sour cream
salt and pepper to taste

Line two 9" pie plates with one crust each; set aside. Combine chicken, onion, soups, sour cream, and salt and pepper to taste in a large bowl; mix well. Divide between bottom pie crusts; top with remaining crusts. Crimp crusts to seal and cut several slits in top. Bake at 350 degrees for 35 to 45 minutes, until bubbly and crusts are golden. Makes 2 pies, 6 servings each.

Donna Riggins
Albertville, AL

no time to thaw?

Use refrigerated pie crusts instead of frozen. Look for them near prepared cookie dough and biscuits at the grocery store.

Chicken & Sausage Skilletini

¼ c. olive oil
2 boneless, skinless chicken
    breasts, cubed
½ lb. spicy ground pork sausage
1 red onion, thinly sliced
2 cloves garlic, minced
14½-oz. can diced tomatoes
1 red pepper, sliced

3 T. brown sugar, packed
1 t. dried basil
½ t. dried oregano
⅛ t. salt
⅛ t. pepper
16-oz pkg. linguine pasta,
    cooked
Optional: fresh oregano leaves

"I like to serve this hearty one-pan dish with French bread and olive oil for dipping."

—Elizabeth

Heat oil in a large skillet over medium heat. Add chicken, sausage, onion and garlic; cook until juices run clear when chicken is pierced. Add tomatoes, red pepper, brown sugar, basil, oregano, salt and pepper; simmer 5 minutes. Add cooked pasta and simmer an additional 5 minutes. Garnish with oregano, if desired. Serves 4 to 6.

Elizabeth Cisneros
Chino Hills, CA

Bacony Chicken

Choose hickory-smoked bacon for extra flavor.

6 slices bacon, crisply cooked
    and crumbled, drippings
    reserved
1 T. butter
1 T. olive oil
6 boneless, skinless chicken
    breasts

1 onion, chopped
3 cloves garlic, minced
½ t. salt
⅛ t. pepper
1½ c. shredded Cheddar cheese

Combine reserved bacon drippings, butter and oil in a large skillet over medium heat. Add chicken and cook until juices run clear when chicken is pierced, turning once. Remove chicken from skillet; place in an ungreased 13"x9" baking pan and set aside. Add onion and garlic to skillet; cook until onion is soft. Stir in salt, pepper and crumbled bacon. Spoon onion mixture over chicken; sprinkle with cheese. Bake, uncovered, at 350 degrees for 10 to 15 minutes, until cheese melts. Serves 6.

Annette Ingram
Grand Rapids, MI

save the drippings

Never put bacon drippings down the disposal. Instead, fill a glass jar with leftover drippings and keep them covered in the refrigerator. Use in place of butter or oil to add a rich, smoky flavor.

Potluck Poppy Seed Chicken

This easy-to-make favorite tastes great!

4 boneless, skinless chicken
    breasts, cooked and cubed
10¾-oz. can cream of chicken
    soup
8-oz. container sour cream
½ c. butter, melted
1 sleeve round buttery crackers,
    crushed
2 T. poppy seed

Stir together chicken, soup and sour cream in a lightly greased 8"x8" baking pan. Mix butter, crackers and poppy seed; spread mixture over chicken. Bake, uncovered, at 350 degrees for 30 minutes, or until bubbly. Serves 4.

Jennifer Langley
Kannapolis, NC

flatten 'em first!

Boneless chicken and pork slices cook up in a jiffy when they're flattened first. Get a rubber mallet from the hardware store just for this purpose. Its soft surface won't tear the wax paper or plastic wrap like a metal meat mallet will.

Creamy Turkey Lasagna

Use leftover turkey from family holiday feasts to make this delicious casserole.

10¾-oz. can cream of mushroom
   soup
10¾-oz. can cream of chicken
   soup
1 c. grated Parmesan cheese
1 c. sour cream
¼ c. chopped pimento

2 to 3 c. cooked turkey, chopped
1 c. onion, chopped
½ t. garlic salt
8-oz. pkg. lasagna noodles,
   cooked
2 c. shredded Cheddar cheese
Garnish: torn fresh parsley

"Once you taste this family favorite, you'll make it all the time!"

—Jennifer

Combine soups, Parmesan cheese, sour cream, pimento, turkey, onion and garlic salt in a large bowl; mix well. Spread one-fourth of turkey mixture on the bottom of a lightly greased 13"x9" baking pan; place noodles on top. Alternate layers of remaining turkey and noodles; top with Cheddar cheese. Bake, uncovered, at 350 degrees for 40 to 45 minutes. Let stand 10 minutes before serving. Garnish with parsley. Serves 8.

Jennifer Eveland
Blandon, PA

use your headscarf...

Bright bandannas make colorful napkins. Find them in shades of blue, pink, yellow, red and green. Tie one around each set of flatware for lap-size napkins. Then, after dinner, toss them in the washer...so easy!

Ham & Potato Casserole

Using prepared or leftover mashed potatoes makes this even quicker!

1 c. green pepper, chopped
½ c. onion, chopped
¼ c. butter
10¾-oz. can cream of mushroom
    soup
¾ c. milk

1 T. mustard
½ t. pepper
5 c. cooked ham, cubed
24-oz. pkg. prepared mashed
    potatoes
Garnish: minced fresh parsley

Sauté green pepper and onion in butter in a large skillet over medium-high heat 5 minutes, or until tender; add remaining ingredients except mashed potatoes and parsley. Bring to a boil; remove from heat and pour into a greased 2-quart casserole dish. Arrange mashed potatoes in a ring on top. Bake, uncovered, at 350 degrees for 20 minutes. Garnish with parsley. Serves 6.

Sally Jukola
Manitou Springs, CO

already whipped

Save recipe prep time by picking up beaten eggs in the dairy department. Great for dinner recipes, they also make quick work of scrambled eggs for breakfast!

Good Morning Sausage Casserole

8-oz. tube refrigerated crescent rolls
6 eggs, beaten
¼ c. milk
salt and pepper to taste
1 lb. ground pork breakfast sausage, browned and drained
2 c. shredded Cheddar cheese

Unroll crescent rolls into the bottom of a greased 13"x9" baking pan. Spoon browned sausage over rolls. Combine eggs, milk, salt and pepper in a bowl and beat well; pour over sausage. Sprinkle cheese on top. Bake, uncovered, at 350 degrees for 25 to 30 minutes. Serves 15.

Beth Bundy
Long Prairie, MN

"I received this hearty all-in-one breakfast recipe from an old friend...it's become a family favorite!"

—Beth

Cheesy Bacon Casserole

This casserole is just the right size for a small family. Double the recipe to feed a crowd.

4 slices white bread, crusts trimmed	¼ t. dried, chopped onion
8 slices bacon, crisply cooked and crumbled	1 c. shredded Cheddar cheese
4 eggs, beaten	
1½ c. milk	
1 t. dry mustard	

Arrange bread slices in a lightly greased 8"x8" baking pan; set aside. Stir together eggs, milk, mustard and onion; pour over bread. Sprinkle with bacon; cover and refrigerate 8 hours or overnight. Let stand at room temperature 30 minutes; uncover and bake at 350 degrees for 20 minutes. Sprinkle with cheese and bake an additional 5 minutes, or until cheese melts. Serves 4.

Laura Strausberger
Roswell, GA

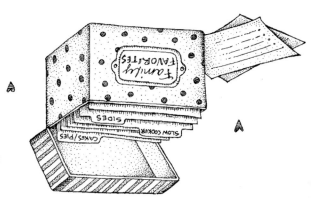

make it a recipe swap

Have potluck guests send you the recipes they are making so no one makes the same thing. Print recipe cards for each dish and hand them out as party favors.

Cheesy Ham Strata

Put together the night before, this makes a great dish for celebrations and brunch!

12 slices bread, crusts trimmed
¾ lb. Cheddar cheese, sliced
10-oz. pkg. frozen chopped
    broccoli, cooked
2 c. cooked ham, cubed
2 T. dried, minced onion

6 eggs, beaten
3½ c. milk
½ t. salt
¼ t. dry mustard
½ c. shredded Cheddar cheese

Cut out desired shapes from center of each bread slice using cookie cutters; set aside the cut-out shapes and place the remaining bread in a greased 13"x9" baking pan. Layer Cheddar cheese slices over bread pieces; spread broccoli and ham over cheese slices. Sprinkle with onion; arrange cut-out shapes on top. Combine eggs, milk, salt and mustard in a bowl and blend well; pour over top of strata. Cover and refrigerate overnight; bake, uncovered, at 325 degrees for one hour 5 minutes, or until set, sprinkling with shredded Cheddar cheese the last 5 minutes of baking. Let stand 10 minutes before serving. Serves 8.

Vivian Baker
Centerville, OH

Spicy Sausage & Rice

Turn a packaged mix into a hearty, delicious main dish.

1 lb. hot ground pork sausage
1 onion, diced
Optional: 1 green pepper, diced

6.9-oz. pkg. chicken-flavored
   rice vermicelli mix
2½ c. water

Cook sausage in a skillet over medium heat until almost browned; add onion and green pepper, if using. Continue to cook until sausage is thoroughly cooked and onion is tender; drain. Add seasoning packet from rice mix; stir well. Add rest of rice mix; sauté 3 to 4 minutes, stirring frequently. Add 2½ cups water and bring to a boil. Cover and reduce heat; simmer 20 to 25 minutes, until rice is tender. Serves 4.

Mildred Dearden
Scott City, KS

Italian Crescent Casserole

My family truly enjoys this crust-topped casserole…we like it better than spaghetti!

1½ to 2 lbs. ground beef or turkey
1 onion, chopped
16-oz. jar spaghetti sauce
8-oz. pkg. shredded mozzarella cheese

8-oz. container sour cream
8-oz. tube refrigerated crescent rolls
2 T. butter, melted
½ c. grated Parmesan cheese

Brown meat and onion in a large skillet over medium heat. Drain and blot with paper towels; return to skillet. Stir in sauce; simmer about 10 minutes. Spoon mixture into a greased 13"x9" baking pan. Combine mozzarella cheese and sour cream; spoon over mixture in pan. Unroll crescent rolls but do not separate; place on top of mixture in pan. Drizzle rolls with melted butter; sprinkle with Parmesan cheese. Bake, uncovered, at 350 degrees for 30 minutes, or until bubbly and golden. Serves 8.

Amanda Gladden
Oneonta, AL

Zesty Pizza Casserole

Add your favorite pizza topping to this easy casserole.

1 lb. ground beef
½ c. onion, chopped
½ c. green pepper, chopped
2 16-oz. cans pizza sauce
4-oz. can mushrooms, drained
4-oz. pkg. sliced pepperoni
½ t. salt
½ t. dried oregano
½ t. garlic powder
½ t. dried basil
2 c. cooked elbow macaroni
¾ c. shredded mozzarella cheese
Garnish: sliced fresh basil

Brown ground beef with onion and green pepper in a large skillet over medium heat; add remaining ingredients except mozzarella cheese and garnish. Pour into a lightly greased 2-quart casserole dish; sprinkle with cheese. Bake, uncovered, at 350 degrees for 30 to 45 minutes. Garnish with basil. Serves 4 to 6.

Valerie Neeley
Robinson, IL

fun with dinner...

Host family game night. Let the kids help prepare dinner and set up games they would like to play when the dishes are done.

Southwestern Casserole

The kids will love this...and the grown-ups too!

2 lbs. ground beef
1 onion, chopped
2 10-oz. cans enchilada sauce
2 16-oz. cans chili beans with
    sauce
13½-oz. pkg. tortilla chips,
    divided

8-oz. pkg. shredded Cheddar
    cheese
Garnish: sour cream, chopped
    fresh cilantro

Brown beef and onion in a skillet over medium heat; drain. Stir in enchilada sauce and beans. Coarsely break up tortilla chips, reserving ½ cup. Arrange remaining chips in a lightly greased 13"x9" baking pan; spread meat mixture on top. Sprinkle with reserved ½ cup tortilla chips and Cheddar cheese. Bake, covered, at 350 degrees for 30 minutes. Remove from oven. Serve immediately, garnished with sour cream and cilantro. Serves 6.

Bobbi Carney
Arvada, CO

Cheesy Chili Bake

1 lb. ground beef
1 c. onion, chopped
1¼-oz. pkg. chili seasoning mix
14½-oz. can diced tomatoes with jalapeños
15-oz. can corn, drained
15-oz. can kidney beans, drained and rinsed
1 c. corn or tortilla chips, crushed
1 c. shredded Colby Jack cheese
Garnish: sour cream

Brown beef and onion in a large skillet over medium heat; drain. Add chili seasoning mix, tomatoes, corn and beans; cook until heated through, stirring occasionally. Spoon mixture into a lightly greased 8"x8" baking pan. Top with crushed chips and cheese. Bake, uncovered, at 350 degrees for 20 minutes, or until cheese melts. Garnish with dollops of sour cream. Serves 4 to 6.

Kathy Huff
Kingsport, TN

round out the meal

Serve this yummy dish with a side of fresh cornbread. Try different mix-ins with your batter. Corn kernels, diced jalapeños or chopped green chiles make for an interesting twist.

Tomato-Corn Casserole

For a leaner version, try substituting ground turkey for the ground beef.

1 onion, chopped
1 green pepper, chopped
1 T. olive oil
2 lbs. ground beef
16-oz. pkg. medium egg noodles,
    cooked

14¾-oz. can creamed corn
15-oz. can tomato sauce
1 T. cocktail sauce
1 c. shredded Cheddar cheese

"Egg noodles and a sprinkling of cheese make this a favorite!"

—Karen

Sauté onion and green pepper in oil in a 10" skillet over medium-high heat until tender. Add beef to skillet and cook until browned; remove skillet from heat and drain. Stir in cooked noodles, corn, tomato sauce and cocktail sauce; spoon into a lightly greased 13"x9" baking pan. Bake, uncovered, at 350 degrees for 25 minutes; sprinkle with cheese and bake until cheese melts. Serve warm. Serves 10 to 12.

Karen Holder
Hamilton, OH

Cornbread-Topped Beef Bake

½ lb. ground beef
1 onion, chopped
3 slices bacon, crisply cooked
    and crumbled, drippings
    reserved
10¾-oz. can tomato soup
⅔ c. water
2 16-oz. cans black beans,
    drained and rinsed

1 t. chili powder
½ t. garlic powder
Optional: ¼ t. red pepper flakes
1 c. shredded Cheddar cheese
8½-oz. pkg. cornbread mix
Garnish: shredded Cheddar
    cheese

"Use a cast-iron skillet... just pop it right into the oven for one-pot convenience!"

—Regina

Brown beef and onion in reserved drippings in a large skillet over medium heat; drain. Stir in soup, ⅔ cup water, crumbled bacon, beans, chili powder, garlic powder and red pepper flakes, if using. Simmer over low heat 20 minutes, stirring often and adding a little more water, if needed. Sprinkle one cup Cheddar cheese over beef mixture; mix well. Pour into a lightly greased 13"x9" baking pan; set aside. Prepare cornbread batter, according to package directions, and spread over beef mixture. Bake, uncovered, at 400 degrees for 20 to 30 minutes, until cornbread is golden. Garnish with additional Cheddar cheese. Serves 6.

Regina Vining
Warwick, RI

Dilly Egg Salad
Sandwiches, page 141

Chunky Gazpacho,
page 122

savory
soups &
sandwiches

Here's the place for bowls of comfort and layers
of goodness or just a doggone delicious lunch.
Almost-Homemade Tomato Soup (page 123)
does wonders with a few cans from the cup-
board and Lisa's Chicken Tortilla Soup (page
130) is as festive as it is delicious. Delight the
kids with Dressed-Up Dogs (page 150). Bring
a stack of Dilly Egg Salad Sandwiches (page
141), Ranch Chicken Wraps (page 147) or
Beefy Filled Hard Rolls (page 155) to a party...
you're sure to leave with an empty platter!

Chunky Gazpacho

(pictured on page 120)

Fresh tomatoes from the garden make this gazpacho very special. Serve in big, icy mugs garnished with stalks of celery.

2½ c. tomato juice
3 T. lemon juice
¼ c. plus 1 T. olive oil
6 tomatoes, peeled and chopped
2 cucumbers, peeled, seeded and chopped

½ c. green pepper, chopped
½ c. onion, finely chopped
1 clove garlic, minced
hot pepper sauce to taste
salt and pepper to taste

Combine tomato juice, lemon juice and olive oil in a bowl; whisk to mix and set aside. Combine tomatoes, cucumbers, green pepper, onion and garlic in a large bowl; pour dressing over vegetable mixture and mix well. Add hot pepper sauce, salt and pepper to taste. Cover and chill; serve cold. Serves 4.

Almost-Homemade Tomato Soup

Creamy and comforting.

2 T. margarine
1 onion, chopped
1 clove garlic, chopped
8-oz. pkg. cream cheese, softened
1½ t. dried basil

½ t. paprika
1¼ c. milk
2 10¾-oz. cans tomato soup
2 16-oz. cans whole tomatoes

Melt margarine in a large saucepan over medium heat; add onion and garlic and sauté about 2 minutes. Add cream cheese, basil and paprika; cook until creamy, stirring constantly. Gradually whisk in milk and soup. Stir in tomatoes and simmer over low heat 30 minutes, or until heated through. Serves 4.

Sandy Neith
Abilene, TX

out of the pot, into the freezer...

You can freeze most soups in a labeled airtight container for up to 3 months. Just be sure to cool the soup completely before freezing and thaw it completely overnight in the refrigerator before reheating.

Old-Fashioned Veggie Soup

Homestyle taste in half the time!

4 c. beef broth
1¾ c. potatoes, peeled and
   diced
1½ c. onion, chopped
1 c. carrots, sliced
1 c. celery, sliced
½ t. dried basil
½ t. pepper
¼ t. salt
¼ t. dried thyme

2 bay leaves
2 28-oz. cans whole tomatoes,
   undrained
10-oz. pkg. frozen corn,
   partially thawed
10-oz. pkg. frozen baby lima
   beans, partially thawed
10-oz. pkg. frozen sliced okra,
   partially thawed
pepper to taste

Combine beef broth, potatoes, onion, carrots, celery, basil, pepper, salt, thyme and bay leaves in a large stockpot. Place tomatoes in a blender; process until smooth and add to stockpot. Bring to a boil, reduce heat and simmer, covered, 40 minutes. Add corn and lima beans; simmer until tender, stirring occasionally. Add okra and bring to a boil; reduce heat and simmer 5 minutes. Add pepper to taste. Discard bay leaves before serving. Serves 8.

Amy Biermann
Riverside, OH

Dan's Broccoli & Cheese Soup

Make it in a slow cooker and serve with seasoned croutons.

16-oz. pkg. frozen chopped
    broccoli, thawed
10¾-oz. can cream of mushroom
    soup
1 c. milk
1 c. half-and-half

8-oz. pkg. cream cheese, cubed
1½ c. pasteurized process cheese
    spread, cubed
garlic powder to taste
pepper to taste

Combine all ingredients in an ungreased slow cooker; cover and cook on high setting 30 to 40 minutes. Reduce setting to low; cook an additional 3 to 4 hours, stirring occasionally. Serves 6.

Dan Ferren
Terre Haute, IN

"When I was in college, I had an employer who made an out-of-this-world broccoli & cheese soup. Now that I'm a stay-at-home dad, I decided to improvise on what I remembered... my whole family loves it! I think it might even be better than the original, and using a slow cooker makes it even easier."

—Dan

Simple Seafood Chowder

Serve this with a lovely warm crusty bread.

¼ c. butter
1 stalk celery, diced
¼ t. dried thyme
¼ t. pepper
3 T. biscuit baking mix
15-oz. can lobster bisque
2 10¾-oz. cans cream of
   potato soup

3½ c. milk
1½ lbs. seafood (such as shrimp,
   scallops and crabmeat),
   peeled, cleaned and cut
   into bite-size pieces
3 to 4 green onions, thinly sliced

Melt butter in a large heavy saucepan over low heat; sauté celery until tender. Stir in thyme, pepper and baking mix. Add bisque, soup and milk; cook until smooth, stirring constantly. Increase heat to medium; when soup is hot, add seafood, stirring occasionally. About 5 minutes after adding seafood, add green onions; simmer until seafood is thoroughly cooked. Serves 6.

Carol Blessing
Averill Park, NY

Chicken Gumbo

You'll really enjoy this flavorful soup...it will warm you up on a chilly day!

3½-lb. boneless, skinless chicken breasts
4 c. water
⅓ c. onion, chopped
16-oz. can tomatoes
⅓ c. rice, uncooked

salt to taste
2½ t. pepper
3 to 4 c. okra, chopped
1½ c. corn
½ t. dried basil
¼ t. garlic salt

Place chicken and 4 cups water in a Dutch oven. Cover and bring to a boil; reduce heat and simmer one hour, or until chicken is tender and juices run clear when chicken is pierced. Remove chicken from Dutch oven and set aside; when chicken is cool enough to handle, cut into bite-size pieces and refrigerate until ready to use. Chill broth several hours; skim off and discard any fat from top. Stir onion, tomatoes, rice, salt and pepper into broth in Dutch oven. Bring to a boil and simmer 30 minutes. Add chicken and remaining ingredients. Continue to simmer an additional 30 minutes. Serves 7 to 8.

Anna Ogle
Sylacauga, AL

fresh...from the freezer

If fresh okra is not available, you can use frozen as a substitute. Be sure to thaw it completely before adding to the stew.

Lisa's Chicken Tortilla Soup

"I've tossed this soup together on many occasions. It's a snap to make...a real lifesaver when extra people turn up for supper!"

—Lisa

4 14½-oz. cans chicken broth
4 10-oz. cans diced tomatoes
   with green chiles
1 c. canned or frozen corn
30-oz. can refried beans

5 c. cooked chicken, shredded
Garnish: shredded Mexican-
   blend cheese, corn chips or
   tortilla strips, chopped fresh
   cilantro

Combine broth and tomatoes with chiles in a large stockpot and place over medium heat. Stir in corn and beans; bring to a boil. Reduce heat to low and simmer 5 minutes, stirring frequently. Add chicken and heat through. Garnish bowls of soup as desired. Serves 6 to 8.

Lisa Johnson
Hallsville, TX

Italian Sausage Soup

Make this a complete meal with a tossed spinach salad and crusty Italian bread.

2 lbs. Italian turkey sausages, casings removed
1 onion, chopped
3 qts. chicken broth
4 potatoes, peeled and cubed
10-oz. pkg. frozen chopped spinach

2 c. half-and-half
1 c. grated Parmesan cheese
Garnish: additional grated Parmesan cheese

Brown sausage and onion in a large Dutch oven over medium heat; drain. Add broth and potatoes; simmer 15 minutes, or until potatoes are tender. Add frozen spinach and half-and-half; simmer until heated through. Just before serving, stir in one cup Parmesan cheese; garnish each serving with additional Parmesan cheese. Serves 6.

Deb Quillen
Creston, OH

Minestrone Soup

6 slices bacon
1 onion, chopped
1 c. celery, chopped
2 cloves garlic, minced
2 t. fresh basil, chopped
½ t. salt
2 10¾-oz. cans beans and
   bacon soup

2 14½-oz. cans beef broth
2 lbs. canned tomatoes
2 c. zucchini, peeled and
   chopped
2 c. cabbage, chopped
1 c. macaroni, uncooked

"My aunt gave this recipe to me about 20 years ago. It makes a wonderful main-dish soup, and it is very easy to prepare."

—Linda

Place bacon, onion, celery and garlic in a large stockpot over medium heat; cook until bacon is crisp and onion, celery and garlic are tender. Drain drippings; add basil, salt, soup, broth, tomatoes, zucchini, cabbage and macaroni. Fill empty soup can with water 3 times and add to soup. Bring to a boil and cook until macaroni reaches desired doneness. Serves 10 to 12.

Linda Newkirk
Central Point, OR

Corn & Bacon Chowder

For added texture, stir in ½ cup frozen corn kernels and then sprinkle with an extra slice of crisp, chopped bacon to finish. The contrast of sweet corn and smoky bacon makes this delicious comfort food.

"This is my husband's favorite! Sometimes I stir in leftover diced cooked chicken."

—Judy

8 slices bacon, diced
1 c. onion, chopped
4 14.5-oz. cans chicken broth
4 c. potatoes, peeled and diced

4 c. creamed corn
salt and pepper to taste
Garnish: chopped fresh parsley

Cook bacon in a Dutch oven over medium heat until almost crisp; add onion and cook until tender. Add broth, potatoes and corn; cover and bring to a boil. Reduce heat; simmer 12 to 15 minutes, until potatoes are tender. Add salt and pepper to taste; garnish with parsley. Serves 8.

Judy Voster
Neenah, WI

Krysti's Delicious Slow-Cooker Chili

1 lb. ground beef, browned and
   drained
2 28-oz. cans crushed tomatoes
2 15-oz. cans light red kidney
   beans
3 T. dried, minced onion

1 T. chili powder
1 T. sugar or to taste
salt and pepper to taste
Garnish: shredded Cheddar
   cheese, chopped fresh
   parsley

"This chili is always on hand at the Apple Cider Weekend we have in October. Made in a slow cooker...what could be easier?"

—Krysti

Place all ingredients except garnish in an ungreased 4-quart slow cooker. Cover and cook on high setting 4 hours. Garnish with cheese and parsley. Serves 6.

Krysti Hilfiger
Covington, PA

easy add-ons

Serve chili with a variety of toppings such as crackers, sour cream and green onions. Allow guests to help themselves.

Quick & Easy Beef Stew

Stew simmering on the stove…is there anything better?

1 T. vegetable oil
1 lb. boneless beef sirloin steak,
    cut into 1-inch cubes
10¾-oz. can French onion soup

10¾-oz. can tomato soup
1 T. Worcestershire sauce
24-oz. pkg. frozen stew
    vegetables

Heat oil in a large skillet over medium heat and add steak; cook until browned and juices have evaporated, stirring occasionally. Add soups, Worcestershire sauce and vegetables; bring to a boil. Reduce heat; cover and cook over low heat 10 to 15 minutes, until vegetables are tender. Serves 4.

Linda Shively
Hopkinsville, KY

Mom's Eggplant Sandwich

1 eggplant, sliced ½-inch thick
2 zucchini or yellow squash,
    sliced ½-inch thick
salt and pepper to taste
2 T. olive oil
3 to 4 T. mayonnaise

1 French bread baguette, halved
    lengthwise
1 tomato, thinly sliced
¼ c. grated Parmesan cheese,
    divided

Sprinkle eggplant and squash slices with salt and pepper; set aside. Heat oil in a grill pan over medium heat. Grill eggplant and squash until they are tender and have grill marks; place on a paper towel. Spread mayonnaise over cut sides of baguette. Place tomato slices on bottom half; sprinkle with salt, pepper and half of Parmesan cheese and top with grilled eggplant and squash. Sprinkle with remaining cheese and add top half of baguette; slice into quarters. Serves 4.

Ilene Magee
Staunton, VA

"Every time I came home from college, Mom would have these sandwiches ready for me. To this day, I still love them!"

—Ilene

for a family on the go

Make all of the sandwiches, wrap them in aluminum foil and refrigerate. Reheat them in the toaster oven or under the broiler when each family member is ready to eat.

Dilly Egg Salad Sandwiches

(pictured on page 120)

A new twist on an old standby, these are extra cute wrapped in parchment or wax paper and tied with string. Serve with crisp kettle-style potato chips for crunch.

8 eggs, hard-boiled, peeled and chopped
¼ c. mayonnaise
1½ T. Dijon mustard
¼ c. celery, minced
2 T. green onions, minced
2 T. fresh dill, chopped
2 t. white vinegar
salt and pepper to taste
8 slices country-style bread
2 c. shredded lettuce

Combine all ingredients except bread and lettuce in a bowl; mix well and chill. When ready to serve, divide egg salad evenly among 4 slices of bread; top with lettuce and remaining bread slices. Serve immediately. Serves 4.

Dana Cunningham
Lafayette, LA

Black Bean Burgers

"These burgers are very good...and they're healthy for you too. Served with all the fixin's, my kids don't even realize there is no meat inside!"

—Amy

15-oz. can black beans, drained and rinsed
1 onion, chopped
1 egg, beaten
½ c. dry bread crumbs
1 t. garlic salt
1 t. cayenne pepper
4 whole-wheat buns, split
Garnish: sliced tomatoes, Swiss cheese slices

Place black beans and onion in a food processor; process until the mixture is mashed. Place bean mixture in a bowl; add egg, bread crumbs, garlic salt and cayenne pepper and mix well. Shape into 4 patties; cook on a grill or in a skillet over medium-high heat 5 minutes on each side, or until golden. Place burgers on buns; garnish with tomato and cheese slices. Serves 4.

Amy Pierce
Flower Mound, TX

Pita Tuna Melts

This recipe gives an old favorite a new twist.

2 6-inch pita rounds
6-oz. can tuna, drained
1 T. mayonnaise
1 T. dill pickle relish

¼ t. dill weed
⅛ t. salt
½ tomato, cut into thin wedges
½ c. shredded Cheddar cheese

Place pita rounds on an ungreased baking sheet; bake at 400 degrees for 5 minutes, or until lightly toasted. Combine tuna, mayonnaise, relish, dill weed and salt in a small bowl; mix well and spread on pitas. Top with tomato wedges; sprinkle with cheese. Bake an additional 5 minutes, or until cheese melts. Serves 2.

Melody Taynor
Everett, WA

a cheery bouquet

Snip new branches from a pussy willow and pair up with the very first forsythia blooms for a cheery spring bouquet…instead of using a vase, gather the stems in a nostalgic watering tin!

The Ultimate Shrimp Sandwich

Treat your family and friends to this scrumptious recipe.

¾ lb. cooked shrimp, peeled
    and chopped
¼ c. green pepper, chopped
¼ c. celery, chopped
¼ c. cucumber, chopped
¼ c. tomato, diced
¼ c. green onions, chopped

¼ c. mayonnaise
Optional: hot pepper sauce to
    taste
6 split-top rolls, split and lightly
    toasted
2 T. butter, softened
1 c. shredded lettuce

Combine shrimp, vegetables, mayonnaise and hot pepper sauce, if using, in a large bowl; toss well and set aside. Spread rolls evenly with butter; divide lettuce among rolls and top with shrimp mixture. Serves 6.

Karen Pilcher
Burleson, TX

even quicker...

To save time on prep, buy pre-chopped vegetables from the produce department.

Ranch Chicken Wraps

½ t. vegetable oil
4 boneless, skinless chicken
    breasts, cut into strips
2.8-oz. can French-fried onions
¼ c. bacon bits

8-oz. pkg. shredded Cheddar
    cheese
lettuce leaves
8 to 10 8-inch flour tortillas
ranch salad dressing

"My husband and children just love these easy-to-make wraps and request them often."

—Lea Ann

Heat oil in a large non-stick skillet over medium heat. Add chicken and cook until chicken is golden and juices run clear when chicken is pierced. Add onions, bacon bits and cheese to skillet; cook until cheese melts. Place several lettuce leaves on each tortilla and spoon chicken mixture down center; roll up. Serve with ranch salad dressing. Makes 8 to 10 wraps.

Lea Ann Burwell
Charles Town, WV

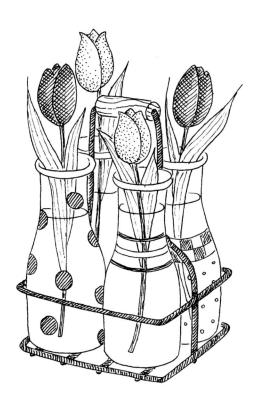

Gobblin' Good Turkey Burgers

"This was my mom's recipe...I'll take these over plain old hamburgers any day!"

—Brandi

1 lb. ground turkey
1 onion, minced
1 c. shredded Cheddar cheese
¼ c. Worcestershire sauce
½ t. dry mustard
salt and pepper to taste
4 to 6 hamburger buns, split

Combine all ingredients except buns in a large bowl and mix well; shape mixture into 4 to 6 patties. Grill over medium-high heat until cooked through and center registers 165 degrees on a meat thermometer. Serve on hamburger buns. Makes 4 to 6 sandwiches.

Brandi Glenn
Los Osos, CA

tasty toppers

Go beyond tomatoes, lettuce and onions. Set out avocado slices, pickled red onions and pineapple slices for a fresh twist.

Deli Skillet Sandwiches

Serve with chips, pickles and vegetable sticks for an easy meal!

4 oz. cooked ham, thinly sliced
4 oz. provolone cheese, thinly
    sliced
4 oz. cooked turkey, thinly sliced

8 slices rye bread
½ c. milk
2 eggs

    Divide ham, cheese and turkey among 4 slices bread. Top with
remaining 4 slices bread and press lightly; cut each sandwich in half
diagonally and set aside. Combine milk and eggs in a shallow bowl
and beat well. Dip each sandwich into egg mixture, coating both sides.
Place a greased skillet over medium heat; add sandwiches and cook
until browned, turning once. Place sandwiches on an ungreased baking
sheet; bake at 400 degrees for 3 to 5 minutes, until cheese melts and
sandwiches are heated through. Makes 4 sandwiches.

Corrine Lane
Marysville, OH

Dressed-Up Dogs

8 hot dogs
8 slices rye bread, toasted
mayonnaise-type salad dressing
  to taste

2 kosher dill pickles, each cut
  lengthwise into 4 slices
4 slices Swiss cheese
Optional: mustard to taste

Slice hot dogs lengthwise, taking care not to cut all the way
through. Place hot dogs cut-side down on a lightly greased hot griddle.
Cook on each side until golden and heated through; set aside. Spread
4 slices bread with salad dressing; top each with 2 pickle slices, 2 hot
dogs and one slice cheese. Spread remaining 4 slices bread with mustard, if using. Place on top of sandwiches. Makes 4 sandwiches.

Shawna Weathers
Judsonia, AR

Slow-Cooker Pulled Pork Sandwiches

Serve with the barbecue sauce of your choice. If hosting others, set out spicy, mild and sweet sauces so guests can choose their favorite.

1 T. vegetable oil
3½ to 4-lb. boneless pork
   shoulder roast, netted or tied
10½-oz. can French onion soup

1 c. catsup
¼ c. cider vinegar
2 T. brown sugar, packed
12 sandwich rolls, split

"Enjoy this Southern-style sandwich like we do...served with coleslaw and dill pickle chips."

—Tina

Heat oil in a skillet over medium heat. Add roast and brown on all sides; place roast in an ungreased slow cooker and set aside. Combine soup, catsup, vinegar and brown sugar in a bowl and mix well; pour over roast. Cover and cook on low setting 8 to 10 hours, until roast is fork-tender. Place roast on a platter; discard string and let stand 10 minutes. Shred roast, using 2 forks; return to slow cooker and stir to mix with sauce. Spoon meat and sauce onto rolls. Serves 12.

Tina Goodpasture
Meadowview, VA

Yummy Blue Cheese Burgers

These mouthwatering burgers will be a hit at your next cookout.

2 lbs. ground beef
Cajun seasoning to taste
1 c. half-and-half
1 clove garlic, finely minced
1 t. dried rosemary
1 t. dried basil

4-oz. container crumbled blue
  cheese
6 kaiser rolls, split, toasted and
  buttered
Optional: sliced mushrooms,
  sliced onion, butter

Shape beef into 6 patties and sprinkle with Cajun seasoning to taste; grill over high heat to desired doneness. Combine half-and-half, garlic and herbs in a saucepan. Bring to a boil and simmer until thickened and reduced by half. Add blue cheese and stir just until cheese melts. Place burgers on rolls; spoon sauce over burgers. If desired, sauté mushrooms and onion in butter until tender; spoon over burgers. Serves 6.

Lynn Daniel
Portage, MI

Beefy Filled Hard Rolls

Sautéed green and red peppers make a savory and colorful topping for these hearty sandwiches.

2 lbs. ground beef
¼ c. onion, diced
10¾-oz. can cream of mushroom
    soup

½ c. Colby cheese, shredded
salt and pepper to taste
12 small French hard rolls, sliced
    and hollowed out

Brown beef and onion in a skillet over medium heat; drain. Add soup and simmer 5 minutes. Stir in cheese, salt and pepper; cook until cheese melts. Fill bottom halves of rolls with beef mixture and cover with top halves. Serves 6.

Diann Stewart
Las Vegas, NV

"Growing up in southern California, we went to the beach a lot. These rolls were one of our favorite things to bring for picnics."

—Diann

Texas Steak Sandwiches

8 slices frozen Texas toast
1½ lbs. deli roast beef, sliced
steak sauce to taste

16 slices provolone cheese
Optional: sautéed green pepper,
  red onion slices

Place Texas toast on an ungreased baking sheet. Bake at 425 degrees for 5 minutes per side, or until softened and lightly golden; set aside. Warm roast beef in a skillet over medium heat until most of juices have evaporated; stir in steak sauce. Place 1 cheese slice on each toast slice. Divide beef evenly among toast slices; top with remaining 8 cheese slices and, if desired, sautéed green pepper and onion slices. Place beef-topped toast on an ungreased baking sheet; bake at 425 degrees until cheese melts. Makes 8 open-faced sandwiches.

Julie Horn
Chrisney, IN

"My husband and I love these hearty sandwiches. They're super simple to make… when guests drop by, I can whip them up in no time, and everyone begs for the recipe."

—Julie

fun finds...

Snap up oversize letters at flea markets and use them to spell out whimsical words such as "EAT" on the dining room wall or "GROW" on a garden fence!

Summer Vegetable
Salad, page 160

splendid
salads &
sides

A potluck just wouldn't be a potluck without an
abundance of sides! Contribute to the spread
with perfect-for-snacking Parmesan Zucchini
Sticks (page 179) or a fresh Ginger-Lime
Salad (page 161) that's sure to stand out from
the crowd. For quick and easy sides, try the
Speedy Baked Beans (page 182) or Super-Fast
Scalloped Potatoes (page 191).

Summer Vegetable Salad

(pictured on page 158)

A "just-right" medley of color, crunch and spice!

Add more or less hot pepper sauce depending on your family's taste preference.

1 c. asparagus, cut into one-inch pieces
1 c. tomatoes, chopped
1 c. zucchini, shredded

1 c. red pepper, diced
2 t. balsamic vinegar
2 T. olive oil
7 dashes hot pepper sauce

Cook asparagus in a saucepan with a small amount of boiling water until crisp-tender. Combine asparagus, tomatoes, zucchini and red pepper in a large bowl; toss to mix. Combine vinegar, oil and hot pepper sauce in a small bowl; whisk until well mixed. Pour dressing over salad and toss to mix. Serves 8.

Ginger-Lime Salad

The surprising taste of peaches makes this a very refreshing salad.

1 head green leaf lettuce, torn
1 peach, pitted and cut into thin
    slices
2 T. fresh parsley, torn
1½ T. fresh ginger, peeled and
    grated

3 T. lime juice
6 T. olive oil
1½ t. honey
salt and pepper to taste

Combine lettuce, peach slices and parsley in a large bowl; toss to mix. Combine ginger, lime juice, olive oil, honey, salt and pepper in a small bowl. Whisk well and pour over lettuce mixture; cover and refrigerate. Serve chilled. Serves 4.

no-fret ginger

Use a zester to grate peeled ginger quickly and efficiently. No zester? Use a food processor.

Three-Bean Basil Salad

Fresh vegetables and basil from your garden will make this wonderful side dish even better!

2 c. canned kidney beans, rinsed
2 c. canned chickpeas, rinsed
2 c. canned green beans, rinsed
1 red onion, sliced and separated
    into rings
1 carrot, peeled and grated
½ c. vinegar

½ c. vegetable oil
6 T. sugar
1 T. fresh basil, minced
¾ t. dry mustard
salt and pepper to taste
Garnish: fresh basil leaves

Combine beans, onion and carrot in a large bowl. Combine remaining ingredients except garnish in a small bowl and mix well; pour over bean mixture and toss well. Cover and refrigerate overnight; serve chilled. Garnish with basil leaves. Serves 10.

what to do with extra basil...

Make your own pesto with this season's leftover basil. Add grated Parmesan cheese, garlic, roasted pine nuts, salt, pepper and olive oil to a food processor. Blend to desired consistency. Freeze pesto in ice cube trays. Use in pastas or as a sauce for baked chicken and fish.

Icebox Slaw

Make this slaw when your garden is bursting with crisp cabbage...and savor it for months to come.

1 head cabbage, shredded
1 t. salt
2 carrots, peeled and grated
1 c. cider vinegar
1 c. sugar
¼ c. fresh parsley, chopped
¼ c. water

Combine cabbage and salt in a large saucepan; cover and let stand one hour. Drain liquid from pan and add carrots. Combine vinegar, sugar, parsley and water in a bowl; whisk until well blended. Pour vinegar mixture over cabbage mixture in pan and toss to mix; place over medium heat and bring to a boil. Cook one minute; remove from heat and cool. Place slaw in airtight containers or plastic zipping bags and freeze up to 3 months; thaw several hours before serving. Serves 6 to 8.

a change of pace

Invite family and friends over for a salad supper. Ask everyone to bring along a favorite salad. You provide crispy bread sticks or a loaf of zucchini bread and a pitcher of iced tea...relax and enjoy!

Cucumber & Tomato Salad

Add more or less Italian salad dressing to suit your taste.

16-oz. pkg. spaghetti, cooked
1 cucumber, peeled and diced
1 tomato, diced
1 onion, diced

¼ c. salad seasoning
8-oz. bottle Italian salad
   dressing

Combine spaghetti, cucumber, tomato, onion and salad seasoning in a large bowl; mix gently. Stir in desired amount of Italian salad dressing; cover and refrigerate. Serve chilled. Serves 10 to 12.

LaVerne Fang
Joliet, IL

Overnight Oriental Salad

For the crunchiest salad, pour dressing over it just before serving!

¾ c. vegetable oil
½ c. sugar
½ c. white vinegar
2 pkgs. Oriental ramen noodles
    with seasoning packets

1 head cabbage, shredded
1 bunch green onions, chopped
1 c. sliced almonds, toasted
1 c. roasted sunflower seeds

Combine oil, sugar, vinegar and seasoning packets from noodles in a bowl and mix well; cover and refrigerate overnight. Crush noodles in a large bowl; add cabbage, green onions, almonds and sunflower seeds. Pour oil mixture over top and toss gently. Serves 10 to 12.

Michelle Allman
Seymour, IN

use your heads

For added color, use a half head each of red cabbage and green cabbage.

Tortellini Salad

"When I need a dish to take to a potluck, this is the one I turn to."

—Mary

2 9-oz. pkgs. cheese and herb
   tortellini, cooked
6-oz. pkg. sliced pepperoni
14-oz. can artichoke hearts,
   quartered

12-oz. can black olives, halved
¼ to ½ c. Italian salad dressing
Garnish: chopped fresh parsley

Combine tortellini, pepperoni, artichokes and black olives in a large bowl; add salad dressing and toss well. Cover and refrigerate at least 2 hours before serving. Garnish with fresh parsley. Served chilled. Serves 6 to 8.

Mary Kitz
Waterville, OH

Sesame Broccoli Sauté

1 T. sesame oil
2 c. chopped broccoli
1 T. sesame seeds

1 green pepper, cut into
¼-inch strips

Heat one tablespoon oil in a large skillet over medium heat; add broccoli and sesame seeds. Sauté 2 minutes; add green pepper and cook until crisp-tender. Serves 4.

Stacie Mickley
Delaware, OH

fresh...or frozen?

Fresh vegetables are delicious and nutritious if they're used promptly, but don't hesitate to use frozen vegetables instead. Flash-frozen soon after being harvested, frozen veggies retain nutrients and are a real time-saver too. Microwave them or add them, still frozen, to a simmering pot of soup or a boiling pasta pot.

Garlicky Spinach

A super-easy, garden-fresh side.

1 T. vegetable oil
2 to 4 cloves garlic, thinly sliced
14-oz. pkg. baby spinach

salt to taste
Garnish: sliced green onions

Combine oil and garlic in a large skillet over low heat; cook 3 minutes, or until garlic is tender, stirring constantly. Add spinach; cover and cook 3 to 4 minutes. Remove from heat and toss well; cover and let stand 2 minutes. Add salt to taste; garnish with green onions. Serves 4 to 6.

Barb Stout
Delaware, OH

shrinking spinach

Spinach has a very high water content. Don't be alarmed when you use the whole package of spinach; the cooking process removes the water, causing the leaves to shrivel and shrink.

Roasted Red, Green & Yellow Peppers

These stuffed roasted peppers are as tasty as they are colorful.

2 green peppers
2 red peppers
2 yellow peppers
3 T. olive oil
3 c. green onions, diced

3 4-oz. pkgs. sliced mushrooms
1 T. fresh thyme, chopped
¾ c. couscous
6 T. water
6 plum tomatoes, chopped

Cut off top third of each pepper and discard; remove seeds and rinse peppers well. Heat oil in a large skillet over medium-high heat. Add green onions and mushrooms and sauté 5 minutes. Add thyme, couscous and water; blend well. Remove from heat and stir in tomatoes. Stuff peppers with couscous mixture and place in a lightly greased baking pan. Bake at 400 degrees for 35 minutes, or until peppers are tender. Serves 6.

Parmesan Zucchini Sticks

Serve these tasty zucchini sticks instead of French fries alongside cheeseburgers...kids will gobble them up!

1 egg
½ c. Italian-flavored dry bread
    crumbs
½ c. grated Parmesan cheese
1 t. dried thyme
½ t. pepper
6 small zucchini, quartered
    lengthwise
ranch salad dressing

    Place egg in a shallow bowl and beat well; set aside. Mix bread crumbs, cheese, thyme and pepper in a separate bowl. Dip zucchini pieces into egg and then into bread crumb mixture; place on a lightly greased baking sheet. Bake at 450 degrees for 20 to 25 minutes, until tender. Serve with ranch salad dressing for dipping. Serves 4.

Marion Sundberg
Ramona, CA

Country-Time Green Beans

The secret to perfect green beans every time? Don't snap off the ends of fresh green beans until they've been cooked and cooled.

1 lb. green beans
1 T. butter
1 T. all-purpose flour
¾ t. sugar
⅓ c. chicken broth, warmed

¾ t. cider vinegar
pepper to taste
3 slices bacon, crisply cooked
    and crumbled

Place green beans in a saucepan and add water to cover; bring to a boil and cook, uncovered, 2 minutes. Drain; plunge beans into cold water and drain again. Cut stems and ends off beans and set aside. Melt butter in a 12" skillet over medium heat; add flour and whisk until smooth. Combine sugar and warm broth in a small bowl, stirring until sugar dissolves; add to flour mixture and mix well. Bring to a boil; cook one minute, stirring constantly. Reduce heat; stir in vinegar and season with pepper. Add beans and bacon and cook until heated through. Serves 6.

Sheri Fuchser
Belton, MO

dunk those beans!

Plunging the green beans into ice-cold water helps them maintain their bright green color and crisp texture.

Speedy Baked Beans

This recipe is amazing! It takes only 10 minutes in the microwave, yet the beans taste like they've been slow-baked for hours.

"To deepen the smoky pork flavor, cook the onion 2 to 3 minutes in bacon drippings before adding to the mixture."

—**Mari**

16-oz. pkg. bacon, crisply cooked and crumbled
2 15-oz. cans pork & beans
1 onion, finely chopped
¼ c. brown sugar, packed

¼ c. maple syrup
¼ c. catsup
½ t. dry mustard
¼ to ½ t. cayenne pepper

Combine all ingredients in an ungreased microwave-safe 3-quart casserole dish and mix well. Cover and microwave on high 10 minutes. Stir before serving. Serves 6 to 10.

Mari Bochenek
Lacey, WA

Vegetable Bake

¼ c. butter
13¼-oz. can mushroom pieces, drained
1 onion, diced
10¾-oz. can cream of mushroom soup
10¾-oz. can cream of chicken soup
11-oz. can cut green beans, drained

11-oz. can yellow wax beans, drained
11-oz. can sliced carrots, drained
8-oz. pkg. shredded Cheddar cheese
8-oz. pkg. shredded mozzarella cheese

Melt butter in a large skillet over medium-high heat; add mushrooms and onion and sauté until golden. Add soups, beans and carrots; cook until heated through. Spread mushroom mixture into a lightly greased 13"x9" baking pan. Sprinkle cheeses on top. Bake, uncovered, at 350 degrees for 30 minutes, or until bubbly. Serves 12 to 15.

Glory Bock
Lee's Summit, MO

check your produce drawer...

Use whatever veggies you have on hand for this easy casserole. Zucchini, squash or eggplant would be a great addition to this hearty bake.

Corn Soufflé

This super-simple dish can be assembled in a flash.

¼ c. margarine
¼ c. all-purpose flour
2 T. sugar
1 t. salt

1¾ c. milk
3 eggs, beaten
3 c. frozen corn, cooked and
    drained

Place margarine, flour, sugar and salt in a saucepan; add milk. Cook and stir over medium heat until thickened; remove from heat. Stir in eggs and corn; pour into a greased 1½-quart casserole dish. Bake, uncovered, at 350 degrees for 45 minutes. Serves 4 to 6.

edible centerpiece

A simple crockery bowl filled to the brim with ripe pears, apples and other fresh fruit makes an oh-so-simple centerpiece...it's a great way to encourage healthy snacking too.

Mesa Corn Pie

14¾-oz. can creamed corn
¼ c. milk
2 c. corn muffin mix
1 c. shredded Cheddar cheese
4½-oz. can diced green chiles,
    drained

3.8-oz. can sliced black olives,
    drained
2 T. butter

"This delicious warm dish has become a tradition in our home."

—Diane

Pour corn into a greased 9"x9" casserole dish; add milk and mix well. Stir in corn muffin mix, Cheddar cheese, chiles and olives; mix well. Dot top with butter; bake, uncovered, at 350 degrees for 35 minutes. Cool 10 minutes before serving. Serves 6 to 8.

Diane Visser-Johnston
Van Nuys, CA

Creamy Herbed New Potatoes

Try this terrific new version of scalloped potatoes!

2 T. butter, divided
½ lb. new potatoes, cut into
    thin slices
1 T. all-purpose flour

2 t. fresh sage, chopped
¼ c. Stilton or feta cheese
⅔ c. half-and-half

Butter an 8"x8" baking pan with ½ tablespoon butter. Place one-third each of potato slices, flour, sage, cheese and half-and-half in pan; repeat layers 2 more times. Dot top with remaining 1½ tablespoons butter. Bake, uncovered, at 350 degrees for 1½ hours, or until golden. Serves 2.

change the cheese

Substitute ¼ cup garlic-and-herbs spreadable cheese for the Stilton or feta for a milder version of this satisfying side dish.

Sweet Potato Casserole

3 c. canned sweet potatoes,
   drained and mashed
8-oz. can crushed pineapple
1 c. sugar
½ c. chopped pecans
1 c. milk

2 eggs, beaten
½ c. all-purpose flour
½ c. butter
1 c. brown sugar, packed
1 c. whole pecans

"My grandmother always
made this yummy dish
for our family, and now
my mom makes it for the
holidays."

—Paula

Combine sweet potatoes, pineapple, sugar, ½ cup chopped pecans, milk and eggs in a large bowl and mix well; spread into a greased 2-quart casserole dish and set aside. Combine flour, butter, brown sugar and one cup whole pecans in a saucepan over low heat; cook until butter melts and sugar dissolves. Pour over sweet potato mixture and bake, uncovered, at 350 degrees for 30 minutes. Serves 8 to 10.

Paula Eggleston
Knoxville, TN

Super-Fast Scalloped Potatoes

3 T. butter
2 T. all-purpose flour
2 c. milk
salt and pepper to taste
4 c. potatoes, peeled and sliced

½ onion, minced
Optional: cubed cooked ham,
    shredded Cheddar cheese
Garnish: sliced green onions

Place butter in a large microwave-safe bowl. Microwave on high 15 seconds, or until melted; add flour and whisk until smooth. Slowly stir in milk; add salt and pepper and stir well. Cover and microwave on high 8 to 10 minutes, until mixture begins to thicken, stirring after 4 minutes. Add potatoes and onion; cover tightly and microwave on high about 15 minutes. Stir in ham and cheese, if using; cover and microwave an additional 2 to 3 minutes, until potatoes are tender. Garnish with green onions. Serves 6 to 8.

Lou Ann Peterson
Frewsburg, NY

"Believe it or not, I prefer this recipe to the old-fashioned way my grandmother used to make scalloped potatoes...I can't say that about many modern recipes!"

—Lou Ann

Paula's Twice-Baked Potatoes

Top with a dollop of sour cream and a sprinkle of snipped fresh chives…heavenly!

6 potatoes
¼ c. butter, softened
½ c. milk
1 onion, finely chopped
6 slices bacon, crisply cooked
    and crumbled

1 t. salt
½ t. pepper
1½ c. shredded Cheddar cheese,
    divided
Optional: sour cream, chopped
    fresh chives

Bake potatoes at 375 degrees for one hour, or until tender; cool. Cut each potato in half lengthwise and scoop out insides, leaving a thin shell. Mash removed potato with butter in a bowl; add milk, onion, bacon, salt, pepper and one cup cheese and mix well. Spoon mixture into potato shells and place on a lightly greased baking sheet. Bake at 375 degrees for 25 minutes. Top with remaining ½ cup cheese; bake an additional 5 minutes, or until cheese melts. Garnish with sour cream and chopped fresh chives, if desired. Serves 12.

Paula Smith
Ottawa, IL

make in advance

Assemble these potatoes in advance and freeze until ready to bake. Wrap each potato in aluminum foil; freeze in a labeled large plastic zipping bag for up to one month. Remove foil and bake as directed, or until thoroughly heated.

Golden Homestyle Rice

This tasty rice offers a nice change of pace from potatoes.

1 c. long-cooking rice, uncooked
1 T. butter
½ c. green onions, chopped
8-oz. pkg. sliced mushrooms
1½ c. chicken broth
½ c. dry sherry or chicken broth
1 t. salt
1 t. pepper
Garnish: chopped green onions

Pour rice into a greased 11"x7" baking pan; set aside. Melt butter in a medium saucepan over medium heat; add ½ cup chopped green onions and sauté until soft. Add mushrooms; sauté until mushrooms are soft. Add chicken broth, sherry or broth, salt and pepper; bring to a boil. Remove from heat and pour over rice in baking pan. Cover and bake at 375 degrees for 25 to 30 minutes. Garnish with additional green onions. Serves 4.

Marcia Emig
Goodland, KS

Italian Bread,
page 198

bountiful breads

Whether you're headed to brunch at the neighbor's or a dinner potluck, bread is always a welcome addition to the table. Start the morning off right with Tina's Ooey-Gooey Cinnamon Rolls (page 230) or light and citrusy Lemon Tea Bread (page 222). Savory sides such as Rosemary Crisp Bread (page 205) or Diane's Skillet Cornbread (page 208) are sure to be a hit with the guests.

Italian Bread

(pictured on page 196)

2½ c. water
2 envs. active dry yeast
2 t. salt
¼ c. sugar
¼ c. olive oil

7 c. all-purpose flour
¼ c. cornmeal
1 egg white
1 T. cold water

Heat 2½ cups water until very warm, about 110 to 115 degrees. Dissolve yeast in very warm water in a large bowl. Add salt, sugar and oil; stir well. Add flour; mix well. Shape dough into a ball and place in a well-greased bowl, turning to coat top. Cover and let rise one hour, or until double in bulk; punch dough down. Divide dough into 3 equal parts and shape into loaves. Place loaves crosswise on a greased baking sheet that has been sprinkled with cornmeal. Cover and let rise 30 minutes. Make 4 diagonal slices in top of each loaf. Bake at 400 degrees for 25 to 30 minutes. Combine egg white and one tablespoon cold water in a small bowl; whisk well and brush on top of loaves. Bake 5 more minutes. Makes 3 large loaves.

Francie Stutzman
Dalton, OH

more than you need?

Make smaller loaves by dividing the dough into six equal parts and baking them for a shorter amount of time. Freeze or give away any you won't use in a week.

Easy Brown Bread

This hearty old-fashioned bread is best hot from the slow cooker, topped with lots of creamy butter. Mmm!

2 c. whole-wheat flour
1 c. all-purpose flour
1 T. baking powder
1 t. salt

2 T. molasses
2 T. vegetable oil
1⅓ c. water

Combine flours, baking powder and salt in a large bowl; stir to mix. Add molasses, oil and 1⅓ cups water; mix until moistened. Place batter in a greased 5-quart slow cooker. Place 5 paper towels across top of slow cooker to catch any condensation. Cover, placing a wooden toothpick between paper towels and lid to allow steam to escape. Cook on high setting 2 hours; do not uncover while cooking. Loosen sides of bread with a knife; remove from slow cooker and place on a wire rack. Makes one loaf.

Tiffany Brinkley
Broomfield, CO

functional & fashionable

Bring a bread basket to your next gathering. Find inexpensive wicker baskets at arts and crafts stores. Line with a patterned dish towel and fill with a variety of bread. It is sure to be a hit!

Herb Garden Bread

Enjoy this braided bread warm from the oven with butter.

When substituting fresh herbs for dried, use three times the amount of dried herbs called for. Dried herbs have a more concentrated flavor, but using fresh herbs adds fresh taste and brighter color.

3 to 4 c. all-purpose flour, divided
3 T. sugar
2 envs. active dry yeast
1½ t. salt
¼ t. dried marjoram, crushed
¼ t. dried thyme, crushed

½ c. water
¼ c. milk
¼ c. butter
1 egg
1 T. butter, melted

Combine 1½ cups flour, sugar, yeast, salt, marjoram and thyme in a large bowl; mix well. Combine ½ cup water, milk and ¼ cup butter in a small saucepan over medium heat. Heat until very warm, about 120 to 130 degrees; add to flour mixture and mix well. Add egg and enough of the remaining flour to make a soft dough. Turn dough out onto a lightly floured surface and knead 5 minutes, adding more flour if needed to prevent dough from sticking. Place dough in a lightly greased bowl; turn to coat top. Cover and let rise until double in bulk. Punch down dough and place on a lightly floured surface. Separate dough into 3 sections and let stand 10 minutes. Roll each section into a 30-inch rope; braid the 3 ropes together and form into a circle, pinching ends together to seal. Place on a lightly greased baking sheet; cover and let rise until double in bulk. Bake at 375 degrees for 30 minutes, covering with aluminum foil if necessary to prevent browning. Brush with one tablespoon melted butter and cool before slicing. Makes one loaf.

Fry Bread

4 c. all-purpose flour
2 T. plus 2 t. baking powder
2 t. salt

1 to 1½ c. milk or water
2 T. shortening

Combine flour, baking powder and salt in a large bowl. Stir to mix; add milk or water and mix well to make a soft dough. Melt shortening in a large skillet over medium heat. Drop dough by spoonfuls into hot shortening; flatten to about ¾-inch thick and cook on both sides until golden. Makes 8 to 10.

Alice Schrader
Covington, IN

Mother's Pull-Apart Cheese Bread

1 loaf unsliced white bakery
  bread
8-oz. pkg. shredded pasteurized
  process cheese spread or
  shredded Mexican blend
  cheese

½ c. butter, softened and
  divided
1½ t. onion, finely chopped
1 t. Worcestershire sauce
¼ t. celery seed
Optional: chopped fresh parsley

Trim crust off top and sides of loaf using a long serrated knife. Without cutting through bottom crust, slice loaf crosswise and lengthwise at 1½-inch intervals to form a loaf of connected 1½-inch cubes. Combine cheese, ¼ cup butter, onion, Worcestershire sauce and celery seed in a bowl and mix well; dab between bread squares. Melt remaining ¼ cup butter; brush over top and sides of loaf. Place on an ungreased baking sheet. Bake at 350 degrees for 20 to 25 minutes, until hot and golden. Garnish with parsley, if desired. Serve immediately. Serves 10 to 12.

Lori Vincent
Alpine, UT

"My mother always made this cheese bread for family get-togethers. Since she is no longer with us, I reach for this buttery, savory bread whenever I need to feel closer to her."

—Lori

Rosemary Crisp Bread

Try cutting this bread into sticks or cubes to dunk in warm soup.

11-oz. tube refrigerated pizza
    crust dough
2 T. Dijon mustard
1 T. garlic, minced
2 t. olive oil

1½ c. shredded Cheddar &
    mozzarella pizza-blend
    cheese
1 t. dried rosemary

    Unroll pizza crust dough on a lightly greased jelly-roll pan; pat out dough to a 12-inch by 10-inch rectangle. Bake at 425 degrees for 5 minutes. Combine mustard, garlic and oil in a small bowl and mix well; spread evenly over baked crust. Sprinkle with cheese and rosemary. Bake 12 to 15 more minutes, until cheese melts and crust is crisp and golden. Serves 10.

Sharon Tillman
Hampton, VA

Cheesy Garlic Bread

¼ c. canola oil
2 T. fresh parsley, minced
1 T. garlic, minced
½ t. salt

¼ t. pepper
1 loaf French or Italian bread,
    halved lengthwise
grated Parmesan cheese to taste

Combine oil, parsley, garlic, salt and pepper in a small bowl; mix well and spread over bread halves. Place bread halves on a lightly greased baking sheet. Bake at 400 degrees for 5 to 8 minutes, until golden. Immediately sprinkle generously with cheese. Cut each bread half into 6 slices. Serves 12.

Gen Mazzitelli
Binghamton, NY

make a difference

Invite friends over for a casual dinner party. Ask guests to bring a nonperishable food item to donate to the local food bank.

Grilled Herb Bread

Try different combinations of herbs...marjoram, chives and basil.

2 c. water
2 envs. active dry yeast
⅓ c. plus 1 t. sugar, divided
⅓ c. vegetable oil

2 t. salt
6 c. all-purpose flour
¼ c. fresh herbs, chopped

Heat 2 cups water until very warm, about 120 to 130 degrees. Combine very warm water, yeast and one teaspoon in a large bowl; let stand 10 minutes. Add remaining ⅓ cup sugar, oil and salt; stir gently to mix. Add 3 cups flour and stir well; gradually add remaining flour, one cup at a time, mixing well. Place dough on a lightly floured surface and knead, adding more flour if needed to prevent dough from sticking. Place dough in a lightly greased large bowl; turn to coat top. Cover and let rise until double in bulk; punch dough down. Lightly grease rolling pin and work surface; cut dough in half and roll out each half to ¼-inch thickness. Lightly grease one side of dough and place on grill over medium-high heat, greased-side down. Lightly grease top side and sprinkle with herbs. Grill 2 minutes; turn and grill 2 more minutes, or until golden. Makes 2 loaves.

indoor barbecue

During the cooler months, heat a grill pan on the stove for the same yummy results as cooking on an outdoor barbecue.

Diane's Skillet Cornbread

If you like a sweet, moist cornbread, you'll love this one!

½ c. butter or margarine
2 8½-oz. pkgs. corn muffin
   mix, divided
⅓ c. sugar

3 eggs, beaten
½ c. milk
Optional: melted butter or
   margarine

Place ½ cup butter or margarine in a 9" cast-iron skillet in a 350-degree oven until melted. Place 1½ packages muffin mix in a large bowl; reserve remaining mix for another use. Add sugar, eggs and milk and mix well. Add melted butter or margarine from skillet; stir well and spoon batter into skillet. Bake at 350 degrees for 30 minutes, or until golden. Brush top with melted butter or margarine, if desired; cut into wedges and serve hot. Serves 8.

Diane Girard
Asheboro, NC

Midwest Cornbread

Stone-ground cornmeal gives this bread a really great texture. Have plenty of sweet butter on hand!

1 c. yellow stone-ground cornmeal
1 c. all-purpose flour
¼ c. sugar

4 t. baking powder
¼ c. vegetable oil
2 eggs
1 c. milk

Grease a 9"x9" baking pan. Combine cornmeal, flour, sugar and baking powder; mix well. Add oil, eggs and milk and mix until smooth. Spoon batter into baking pan. Bake at 425 degrees for 20 minutes, or until golden. Serves 6 to 8.

cast-iron perfection

Use mini cast-iron skillets or cornstick pans to bake perfect individual portions. Baking cornbread in cast iron creates a crisp, golden crust with a moist, soft center.

Cornmeal Biscuits

So tasty with any fish dish! Or serve with butter and strawberry jam for breakfast.

½ c. plus 2 T. fat-free milk
2 T. vegetable oil
1 egg, beaten
1⅓ c. all-purpose flour

⅓ c. cornmeal
1 T. sugar
1½ t. baking powder
¼ t. salt

Top with a fried *egg* and crispy bacon for an *easy* breakfast sandwich!

Combine milk, oil and egg in a small bowl; whisk well. Combine flour, cornmeal, sugar, baking powder and salt in a large bowl; mix well. Add milk mixture, stirring just until moistened. Drop dough by teaspoonfuls onto a lightly greased baking sheet. Bake at 400 degrees for 12 minutes, or until golden. Makes one dozen.

Country Biscuits Supreme

These are good with butter and honey...terrific with beef stew.

2 c. all-purpose flour
4 t. baking powder
2 t. sugar
½ t. salt

½ t. cream of tartar
½ c. shortening
⅔ c. milk

Sift flour, baking powder, sugar, salt and cream of tartar into a large bowl. Cut in shortening until mixture is crumbly. Add milk and stir just until moistened. Turn dough out onto a lightly floured surface; knead gently 30 seconds and roll out to ½-inch thickness. Cut with floured biscuit cutter and place on an ungreased baking sheet. Bake at 425 degrees for 10 to 12 minutes, until golden. Makes 12 to 15.

Gretchen Hickman
Galva, IL

Parmesan Biscuit Bread

Nothing says comfort like warm, fresh-baked bread...and what could be easier than putting your slow cooker to work "baking" it for you?

1½ c. biscuit baking mix
2 egg whites, beaten
½ c. milk
1 T. dried, minced onion

1 T. sugar
1½ t. garlic powder
¼ c. grated Parmesan cheese

Combine all ingredients except Parmesan cheese; stir well. Lightly grease a 2½ to 3-quart slow cooker; spoon dough into slow cooker and sprinkle with cheese. Cover and cook on high setting one to 1¼ hours. Remove from slow cooker and cut into wedges to serve. Makes one loaf.

keep it hot

Try not to open your slow cooker during the cooking process. Removing the lid releases a great deal of heat, which may cause an increase in cook time.

Super-Simple Bread Bowls

For larger bowls, halve the bread dough instead of cutting it into thirds.

2 loaves frozen bread dough   2 eggs, beaten

Thaw bread according to package instructions; cut loaves into thirds and form each into a ball. Place dough balls on lightly greased baking sheets. Cover with lightly greased plastic wrap and let rise until double in bulk. Uncover and brush with beaten eggs. Bake at 350 degrees for 25 minutes, or until golden. Cool. Slice off tops and hollow out bread. Makes 6.

Linda Behling
Cecil, PA

Dot's Popovers

Opening the oven door releases heat and causes popovers to fall, eliminating the light and fluffy texture.

2 eggs, beaten
1 c. milk

1 c. all-purpose flour
½ t. salt

Combine all ingredients in a bowl and mix thoroughly. Spoon batter into well-greased muffin or popover cups, filling ¾ full. Place pan in a cold oven; set temperature to 450 degrees and bake for 30 minutes without opening oven door. Makes 6 to 8.

Nadine Jones
Corinth, ME

"It was always a treat when Gram made her popovers...they are especially good with a bowl of hot chili or stew. Gram always cautioned me not to open the oven while they were baking!"

—Nadine

French Onion Biscuits

These biscuits are quick, easy and scrumptious…wonderful with soups or Italian dishes.

8-oz. container French onion dip
¼ c. milk
1 t. dried parsley

2 c. biscuit baking mix
1 T. butter, melted

Combine onion dip, milk and parsley in a large bowl and mix until smooth. Add baking mix and mix until well blended. Drop dough by spoonfuls onto a lightly greased baking sheet. Bake at 450 degrees for 7 to 8 minutes, until golden. Immediately brush tops of biscuits with melted butter. Makes one dozen.

Lane Ann Miller
Hopkinsville, KY

spice up your butter

Give biscuits an update by serving them with compound butters. Allow one stick of butter to come to room temperature and then mix in your favorite combination of fresh herbs, lemon zest or caramelized onions. Wrap in plastic wrap and refrigerate until ready to serve.

Caraway & Cheddar Scones

Serve these in a pretty napkin-lined basket.

2 c. all-purpose flour
2 t. baking powder
¼ t. salt
6 T. butter
1 c. Cheddar cheese, shredded

1 t. caraway seed
⅓ c. bacon, crisply cooked
   and crumbled
⅓ c. milk
1 egg, beaten

Combine flour, baking powder and salt in a large bowl; stir to mix. Cut in butter until mixture is crumbly; stir in ¾ cup Cheddar cheese, caraway seed and bacon. Combine milk and egg in a small bowl; mix well. Add to flour mixture and mix well. Turn dough out onto a lightly floured surface; knead 5 times and roll to ½-inch thickness. Cut dough with a floured cutter and place on a lightly greased baking sheet. Top scones with remaining ¼ cup cheese and bake at 425 degrees for 15 minutes, or until golden. Makes about 18.

Rosemary-Lemon Scones

Wonderful served warm with butter and jam.

2 c. all-purpose flour
2 T. sugar
1 T. baking powder
2 t. fresh rosemary, chopped
2 t. lemon zest
¼ t. salt

¼ c. butter
2 eggs, beaten
½ c. plus 1 T. whipping cream,
    divided
1 t. cinnamon
1 t. coarse sugar

Combine flour, sugar, baking powder, rosemary, lemon zest and salt in a bowl; mix well. Cut in butter until mixture is crumbly; set aside. Combine eggs with ½ cup whipping cream in a separate bowl and mix well; add to flour mixture and stir. Dough should be sticky. Turn dough out onto a well-floured surface; gently knead 10 times and shape into an 8-inch circle about one-inch thick. Cut circle into wedges and place on a lightly greased baking sheet. Brush with remaining one tablespoon whipping cream. Sprinkle with cinnamon and coarse sugar and bake at 400 degrees for 15 minutes, or until golden. Makes 8.

sub in scones

These scones can be savory or sweet. Try serving for breakfast with butter and a cup of tea, as a stand-in for rolls with roast pork or chicken or with sweetened whipped cream for a satisfying dessert.

Lemon Tea Bread

Make this bread a day ahead to allow time for the flavors to blend.

1 c. sour cream
¾ c. sugar
½ c. butter, softened
2 eggs
1 T. poppy seed

1 T. lemon zest
2 T. lemon juice
2 c. all-purpose flour
1 t. baking powder
1 t. baking soda

Combine sour cream, sugar and butter in a large bowl; mix until fluffy. Add eggs, poppy seed, lemon zest and lemon juice; mix well. Combine flour, baking powder and baking soda in a separate bowl and mix well. Add to egg mixture and mix well. Spoon batter into a greased 9"x5" loaf pan and bake at 325 degrees for one hour, or until a toothpick inserted near the center comes out clean. Cool before slicing. Makes one loaf.

the perfect zest!

Only use the yellow part of the lemon rind when zesting. The white skin or "pith" is bitter and will leave an unpleasant aftertaste. The yellow skin holds the citrus oils that are so flavorful.

Raisin-Cranberry Bread

Lemon Tea Bread

Raisin-Cranberry Bread

(pictured on page 223)

A wonderful combination of flavors!

2 c. all-purpose flour
1 c. sugar
1½ t. baking powder
1 t. salt
½ t. baking soda
¼ c. margarine

1 egg, beaten
1 t. orange zest
¾ c. orange juice
1½ c. golden raisins
1½ c. dried cranberries, chopped

Combine flour, sugar, baking powder, salt and baking soda in a large bowl; cut in margarine until mixture is crumbly. Add egg, orange zest and orange juice. Stir until moist; fold in raisins and cranberries. Pour into a greased 9"x5" loaf pan; bake at 350 degrees for one hour and 10 minutes. Makes one loaf.

Sharon Gailey
Aston, PA

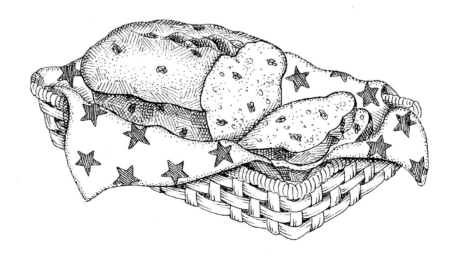

English Crumpets

Simply described, crumpets are cakes cooked on a griddle. A forerunner of the English muffin, they're golden and delicious! Serve with butter, honey or jam.

1½ c. milk
1 c. water, divided
1 env. active dry yeast
2 t. honey

3 c. all-purpose flour
1 t. salt
½ t. baking soda
¼ c. butter, melted

Combine milk and ¾ cup water in a saucepan over high heat and bring to a boil; remove from heat and cool. Add yeast and honey to milk mixture; let stand 5 minutes. Combine flour and salt in a bowl and mix well; add to milk mixture and stir well. Cover and let batter rise one to 2 hours, until double in bulk. Combine baking soda and remaining ¼ cup water in a small bowl; add to batter and mix well. Let batter stand 5 minutes. Brush crumpet rings or large metal cookie cutters and a griddle or large non-stick skillet with melted butter; place rings or cutters on griddle or skillet over medium heat. Spoon batter into rings or cutters and cook 3 minutes, or until golden. Remove rings or cutters; flip crumpets and cook until golden. Repeat with remaining batter, reheating rings or cutters before filling with batter. Serve warm. Makes about 2 dozen.

Cinnamon-Apple Muffins

These muffins are scrumptious served warm with butter...they make any meal a little more special!

2 c. all-purpose flour
1 T. baking powder
1 t. cinnamon
½ t. allspice
⅛ t. salt
3 T. brown sugar, packed
3 T. butter, melted

¾ c. milk
2 T. mayonnaise
2 apples, peeled, cored and
    grated
⅓ c. raisins
⅓ c. chopped walnuts

Sift flour, baking powder, cinnamon, allspice and salt into a large bowl. Add remaining ingredients and mix well; batter will be thick. Spoon batter into 12 paper-lined muffin cups. Bake at 400 degrees for 20 minutes, or until centers spring back when touched. Remove from pan and cool on a wire rack; serve warm. Makes one dozen.

Linda Davidson
Lexington, KY

dress it up

Bake muffins in decorative cupcake wrappers to make breakfast a special occasion.

Pecan Pie Muffins

1 c. chopped pecans
1 c. brown sugar, packed
½ c. all-purpose flour

2 eggs
½ c. butter, melted and cooled
  slightly

Combine pecans, brown sugar and flour in a large bowl and mix well; make a well in the center and set aside. Lightly beat eggs in a separate bowl; stir in butter and mix well. Add to pecan mixture, stirring just until moistened. Grease the bottom of 9 muffin cups; spoon batter into muffin cups, filling ⅔ full. Bake at 350 degrees for 20 to 25 minutes, until golden. Immediately remove from muffin pan; cool on a wire rack. Makes 9.

Melynda Hoffman
Fort Wayne, IN

Soft Gingerbread

Oh-so yummy when you spread warm slices of this tasty bread with whipped butter!

½ c. sugar
1 c. molasses
½ c. butter, softened
2 t. baking soda
1 t. ground ginger

1 t. ground cloves
1 t. cinnamon
1 c. boiling water
2½ c. all-purpose flour
2 eggs, beaten

Combine all ingredients in a large bowl and mix well. Spoon batter into a greased and floured 9"x5" loaf pan. Bake at 350 degrees for 35 to 40 minutes. Makes one loaf.

Holly Sutton
Grahamsville, NY

Tina's Ooey-Gooey Cinnamon Rolls

Use butter-flavored cooking spray when greasing pans used for baking sweets and confections.

"Mmm...mile-high rolls just like we remember from our hometown bakery!"

—Tina

½ c. water
2 envs. active dry yeast
1 c. buttermilk
½ c. plus 3 T. sugar, divided
1 T. salt
4 c. all-purpose flour

4 egg yolks
1½ c. butter, softened and divided
1 T. cinnamon
Optional: ¾ c. raisins

Heat ½ cup water until very warm, about 110 to 115 degrees. Dissolve yeast in very warm water in a large bowl. Add buttermilk, 3 tablespoons sugar, salt, flour, egg yolks and one cup butter; beat with an electric mixer at high speed 8 minutes, or until smooth. Turn out onto an ungreased baking sheet; cover and refrigerate 6 hours. Roll out dough on a floured surface to a 24-inch by 10-inch rectangle (about ½-inch to ¾-inch thick); melt remaining ½ cup butter and brush over dough. Combine remaining ½ cup sugar and cinnamon; mix well and sprinkle over dough. Spread raisins over top, if using; roll up dough jelly-roll style, starting at long edge. Place seam-side down and cut into 2-inch slices. Place on a greased 11"x9" baking sheet; cover and let rise until double in bulk. Bake at 350 degrees for 20 to 25 minutes. Spread Vanilla Glaze over warm rolls. Makes one dozen.

Vanilla Glaze:

1 vanilla bean
2¾ c. powdered sugar
½ c. butter, melted

2 T. water
1 T. vanilla extract

Cut vanilla bean in half lengthwise; scrape out seeds from both halves. Combine vanilla bean seeds, powdered sugar, butter, 2 tablespoons water and vanilla extract in a large bowl and mix until smooth. Makes about 2½ cups.

Tina Stidam
Delaware, OH

Chewy Chocolate Chip
Cookies, page 240

blue-ribbon desserts

Everyone knows that dessert is the best part of the meal, so why not start planning your potluck here? From cookies to pies to cakes and more, these pages are chock-full of scrumptious sweets. Try a twist on pecan pie with Caramel-Pecan Bars (page 243), or bring everyone's favorite...classic Chewy Chocolate Chip Cookies (page 240). Indulge in Triple Fudge Cake (page 261), or cool down with Raspberry Sorbet (page 269).

Cherry Macaroons

1 c. shortening
1 c. sugar
3 eggs
½ c. sour cream
3 c. all-purpose flour
1 t. baking powder

½ t. baking soda
½ t. salt
1 c. shredded coconut
1 t. lemon zest
1½ t. almond extract
⅔ c. candied cherries

Combine shortening, sugar and eggs in a large bowl; mix well and stir in sour cream. Combine flour, baking powder, baking soda and salt in a separate bowl; mix well and add to shortening mixture. Fold in coconut, lemon zest and almond extract. Drop by tablespoonfuls onto ungreased baking sheets. Press one candied cherry into center of each cookie. Bake at 400 degrees for 10 to 12 minutes. Remove from baking sheets; cool on wire racks. Makes 3½ to 4 dozen.

Valerie Thompson

Cinnamon-Sugar Butter Cookies

2½ c. all-purpose flour
½ t. baking soda
¼ t. salt
1 c. brown sugar, packed
½ c. plus 3 T. sugar, divided

1 c. butter, softened
2 eggs
2 t. vanilla extract
1 T. cinnamon

Combine flour, baking soda and salt in a bowl; mix well and set aside. Combine brown sugar and ½ cup sugar in a separate bowl; mix well. Add butter and beat with an electric mixer at medium speed until well blended. Add eggs and vanilla; beat 2 minutes, or until fluffy. Add flour mixture and stir just until blended. Refrigerate dough 30 minutes, or until firm. Shape dough into one-inch balls. Combine remaining 3 tablespoons sugar and cinnamon in a shallow bowl and mix well; roll balls in sugar-cinnamon mixture. Place 2 inches apart on ungreased baking sheets. Bake at 300 degrees for 18 to 20 minutes. Remove from baking sheets; cool on wire racks. Makes 3 dozen.

sweet tooth satisfaction

Host a "Just Desserts" party. Have friends bring over their favorite sweets. Make sure guests bring a variety of cookies, pies and cakes. Serve it all up with glasses of cold milk or mugs of hot chocolate.

Lemon Crunch Cookies

Serve with Blueberry-Lemon Mousse (see page 266) and minty iced tea.

1 c. all-purpose flour	1 t. lemon juice
½ t. baking soda	1 egg
¼ t. cream of tartar	¼ t. allspice
¼ c. margarine, softened	¼ t. salt
¾ c. sugar	1 c. quick-cooking oats,
1 T. lemon zest	uncooked

Combine flour, baking soda and cream of tartar in a bowl and mix well; set aside. Place margarine in a large bowl and beat with an electric mixer at medium speed until creamy; gradually add sugar and beat until well blended. Add lemon zest, lemon juice, egg, allspice and salt; beat well. Gradually add flour mixture and beat until combined. Stir in oats. Drop dough by teaspoonfuls onto lightly greased baking sheets; bake at 350 degrees for 12 minutes. Makes 3½ dozen.

Shareable treats

Share leftover cookies with friends and neighbors. Package cookies in cellophane bags tied with colorful ribbons. Include the recipe on the gift tag.

Gingersnaps

¾ c. butter, softened	2 c. all-purpose flour	"We enjoy these spicy
1 c. sugar	2 t. baking soda	cookies for a cozy
1 egg	1 t. cinnamon	bedtime snack."
½ c. molasses	½ t. salt	—Heidi
2 T. fresh ginger, peeled and grated	additional sugar	

Combine butter and sugar in a large bowl and blend until creamy; add egg and blend until fluffy. Add molasses and ginger; mix well and set aside. Combine flour, baking soda, cinnamon and salt in a separate bowl; mix well and add to butter mixture. Shape dough into one-inch balls. Place additional sugar in a shallow bowl; roll balls in sugar and place on lightly greased baking sheets. Bake at 350 degrees for 10 to 12 minutes; remove from baking sheets and cool on wire racks. Makes about 4 dozen.

Heidi DePriest
Rancho Cucamonga, CA

shape up!

Switch things up by using a variety of cookie cutters. Choose your child's favorite animal or holiday-inspired shapes for a whimsical take on the classic cookie.

Chewy Chocolate Chip Cookies
(pictured on page 232)

¾ c. shortening	1 t. baking soda
1 c. sugar	1 t. salt
1 c. brown sugar, packed	12-oz. pkg. semi-sweet
2 eggs	chocolate chips
1 t. vanilla extract	½ c. pecans, chopped
2½ c. all-purpose flour	

Combine shortening, sugar, brown sugar, eggs and vanilla in a large bowl; mix well. Add flour, baking soda and salt; mix well. Stir in chocolate chips and nuts. Drop by rounded tablespoonfuls onto ungreased baking sheets. Bake at 375 degrees for 10 to 12 minutes; do not overbake. Remove from baking sheets and cool on wire racks. Makes 4 to 5 dozen.

Kathy Zimmerman
Burley, WA

"Whenever I take these to family gatherings, everyone raves about them. My secret...use shortening rather than butter or margarine and don't bake them too long"

—Kathy

make a cake

Create a cookie cake for a loved one's birthday. Bake one giant cookie instead of individual ones. Allow kids to decorate with frosting and candles.

Dulce de Leche Bars

This rich chocolate and caramel dessert makes a wonderful take-along to cookie exchanges and holiday parties! Dulce de leche is caramelized sweetened condensed milk…you'll find it in the Hispanic foods section or with the dessert toppings.

18½-oz. pkg. spice cake mix	14-oz. can dulce de leche
2 eggs, beaten	¼ c. butter
⅓ c. unsweetened applesauce	
6-oz. pkg. semi-sweet chocolate chips	

Combine cake mix, eggs and applesauce in a large bowl; stir until mixture forms a sticky dough. Press three-fourths dough into a lightly greased 13"x9" baking pan; set aside. Place chocolate chips, dulce de leche and butter in a microwave-safe bowl and microwave on high one to 2 minutes, until chips melt. Stir well to combine and spread over dough in pan. Drop large spoonfuls of remaining dough on top of chocolate layer, flattening and spreading as much as possible. Bake at 350 degrees for 20 to 25 minutes, until golden. Cool completely before cutting into bars. Makes 10 to 14.

Andrea Heyart
Aubrey, TX

Caramel-Pecan Bars

16-oz. pkg. yellow cake mix
⅓ c. margarine, softened
2 eggs, divided
14-oz. can sweetened condensed
   milk
1 t. vanilla extract
1 c. chopped pecans
8-oz. pkg. toffee baking bits

Combine cake mix, margarine and one egg in a bowl; mix until crumbly. Pat into a greased 13"x9" baking pan. Combine condensed milk, remaining egg and vanilla in a separate bowl; stir until well blended. Stir in pecans and toffee baking bits. Spread over cake mix mixture. Bake at 350 degrees for 25 to 30 minutes. Cool completely before cutting into bars. Makes 12.

Donna Smith

cool down!

Wait until the bars are completely cool before slicing.
This will ensure pretty squares with perfectly smooth edges.

Hello Dolly Bars

"My sister began making these in the late 1970s, and I make them every time I need a little pick-me-up. My sister is no longer with us, but these wonderful treats hold some very special memories for me, which I have passed down to my children and now my grandson."

—Marilyn

½ c. margarine, melted
1 c. graham cracker crumbs
1 c. sweetened flaked coconut
6-oz. pkg. semi-sweet chocolate chips

6-oz. pkg. butterscotch chips
14-oz. can sweetened condensed milk
1 c. chopped pecans

Combine margarine and graham cracker crumbs in a bowl and mix well; press into a lightly greased 9"x9" baking pan. Top with layers of coconut, chocolate chips and butterscotch chips. Pour condensed milk over top; sprinkle with pecans. Bake at 350 degrees for 25 to 30 minutes. Cool; cut into bars. Makes 12 to 16.

Marilyn Morel
Keene, NH

the right timing...

To avoid overcooking, set your timer for 3 minutes fewer than the allotted time. Ovens can vary in temperature, so checking for doneness a little early will ensure excellent baked goods every time.

Butterscotch Brownies

¼ c. butter
1 c. brown sugar, packed
1 egg
¾ c. all-purpose flour

1 t. baking powder
½ t. salt
½ t. vanilla extract
½ c. chopped nuts

Melt butter in a small saucepan over low heat; remove from heat. Add brown sugar and stir until sugar dissolves; set aside to cool. Add egg and blend well; add flour, baking powder and salt, mixing well. Stir in vanilla and nuts; spread into a greased 8"x8" baking pan. Bake at 350 degrees for 25 minutes; cool before cutting into squares. Makes 9.

Alice Flood
Dallas, TX

Chocolate Éclair Squares

Pop these in the freezer to chill them more quickly!

14.4-oz. box graham crackers
3.9-oz. pkg. instant chocolate
    pudding mix
2 c. plus 3 T. milk, divided
8-oz. container frozen whipped
    topping, thawed and divided

3.4-oz. pkg. instant vanilla
    pudding mix
2 1-oz. sqs. unsweetened
    baking chocolate, melted
6 T. margarine, melted
1½ c. powdered sugar

Line the bottom of an ungreased 13"x9" baking pan with graham crackers; set aside. Combine chocolate pudding mix and one cup milk; mix well and fold in half the whipped topping. Spread chocolate pudding mixture over graham crackers and top with another layer of graham crackers. Repeat using vanilla pudding mix and remaining milk and whipped topping; top with graham crackers. Combine melted chocolate, melted margarine and powdered sugar in a bowl and stir until well mixed; pour over top graham cracker layer. Refrigerate overnight. Cut into squares. Serves 12.

Vickie Haley
Corona, CA

"Store these squares in an airtight plastic container. Place wax paper between layers of bars to prevent sticking."

—Vickie

Apple-Oatmeal Bars

1 c. all-purpose flour
½ c. brown sugar, packed
½ t. salt
½ t. baking soda
1 c. quick-cooking oats,
   uncooked

½ c. shortening
3 red apples, cored and sliced
2 T. butter or margarine
½ c. sugar

Combine flour, brown sugar, salt and baking soda in a large bowl; mix well. Add oats and mix well. Add shortening and mix until crumbly. Spread half of flour mixture in a greased 11"x7" baking pan. Arrange sliced apples over flour mixture; dot with butter or margarine and sprinkle with sugar. Cover with remaining flour mixture, pressing firmly. Bake at 350 degrees for 45 minutes. Cool completely; cut into bars. Makes 8.

Joy Kinnear

bake-sale beauties

When making bar treats for a bake sale, you can dress them up by using shaped cookie cutters to cut them, rolling edges in candy sprinkles or sprinkling lightly with colored sugar.

Mini Apple Hand Pies

1 Granny Smith apple, peeled, cored and finely chopped
¼ c. raisins
3 T. sugar
1 t. cinnamon
12-oz. tube refrigerated biscuits
2 T. butter

Combine apple, raisins, sugar and cinnamon in a bowl; toss to mix and set aside. Flatten each biscuit into a 3-inch circle. Place one tablespoon apple mixture on each biscuit; dot with butter. Bring up sides of biscuit and pinch to seal. Place in ungreased muffin cups. Bake at 375 degrees for 11 to 13 minutes, until golden. Makes 10.

Sheri Dulaney
Englewood, OH

everyday apple pie

Keep a shaker jar of apple pie spice handy if you love to bake. A blend of cinnamon, nutmeg and allspice, it's scrumptious in all kinds of baked goods from pies and cookies to quick breads.

Lemon Sponge Pie

2 T. margarine, softened
1 c. sugar
2 eggs, separated
¼ c. all-purpose flour

⅛ t. salt
zest and juice of one lemon
1 c. milk
9-inch pie crust

Beat margarine in a large bowl with an electric mixer at medium speed until fluffy. Add sugar and egg yolks; beat well. Add flour, salt, lemon zest, lemon juice and milk; beat well. Beat egg whites in a separate bowl at high speed until stiff peaks form; fold into margarine mixture. Pour into pie crust. Bake at 350 degrees for 40 to 45 minutes. Cool and refrigerate; serve chilled. Serves 8.

Vicki Bastian
Mifflinburg, PA

"I cherish this recipe from a grandmother who passed away long before I was born. It makes a wonderful pie with a cakelike bottom and creamy, delicious top."

—Vicki

Peanut Butter Pie

½ c. sugar
½ c. creamy or crunchy
    peanut butter
3-oz. pkg. cream cheese,
    softened

12-oz. container frozen whipped
    topping, thawed
9-inch graham cracker crust
Optional: additional whipped
    cream, chopped peanuts

Combine sugar, peanut butter and cream cheese in a large bowl; stir until well blended. Fold in whipped topping. Spoon mixture into pie crust. Cover and chill at least 2 hours before serving. Top with additional whipped cream and chopped peanuts, if desired. Serves 8.

Carol Nebzydoski
Pleasant Mount, PA

"My kids have always loved this creamy, peanut buttery pie. My 21-year-old son even called from Texas while he was in the army and asked for the recipe so he could make it for a small gathering of friends before they left for Iraq."

—Carol

whipped cream extras

It's easy to save extra whipped cream. Dollop heaping tablespoonfuls onto a chilled baking sheet and freeze. Remove from the baking sheet and store in a plastic zipping bag. To use, place dollops on dessert servings and let stand a few minutes.

Blue-Ribbon Banana Cake

½ c. shortening
¼ c. plus 2 T. butter, softened
    and divided
2 c. sugar, divided
2 eggs
1 c. bananas, mashed
1 c. chopped pecans, divided
2 c. cake flour
1 t. baking soda

1 t. baking powder
¾ t. salt, divided
2 t. vanilla extract, divided
½ c. buttermilk
¼ c. sweetened flaked coconut
½ c. all-purpose flour
½ c. half-and-half
Garnish: sweetened flaked
    coconut

Combine shortening, ¼ cup butter and 1½ cups sugar in a large bowl; beat with an electric mixer at medium speed until fluffy. Add eggs and bananas; beat 2 minutes. Stir in ½ cup pecans. Sift together cake flour, baking soda, baking powder and ½ teaspoon salt; add to shortening mixture. Add one teaspoon vanilla and buttermilk; beat 2 minutes. Divide batter equally between 2 greased and floured 9" round cake pans; sprinkle batter with coconut. Bake at 350 degrees for 25 to 30 minutes. Cool cakes 10 minutes before removing from pans. Combine remaining ½ cup sugar, all-purpose flour, half-and-half and remaining 2 tablespoons butter in a saucepan over medium heat; cook until thickened, whisking frequently. Add remaining ½ cup nuts, ¼ teaspoon salt and one teaspoon vanilla, stirring well; cool. Place first cake, coconut-side down, on a serving platter; spread thickened sugar mixture over top. Place second layer, coconut-side up, over first cake. Swirl on Snow White Frosting, leaving center of cake unfrosted so coconut can be seen. Garnish with additional sweetened flaked coconut. Serves 12 to 16.

Snow White Frosting:

1 egg white
¼ c. shortening
¼ c. butter, softened

¼ t. almond extract
½ t. vanilla extract
2 c. powdered sugar

Combine egg white, shortening, butter and extracts in a large bowl; blend well. Gradually add powdered sugar, beating until fluffy.

Strawberry Angel Cake

Your family & friends will think you're an angel when you serve this cake.

16-oz. baked angel food cake
2 c. whipping cream
⅔ c. strawberry ice-cream
　　topping

2 pts. strawberries, hulled and
　　halved

Slice cake horizontally into 4 layers; set aside. Combine whipping cream and topping in a large bowl and beat with an electric mixer at high speed until stiff peaks form. Place bottom layer of cake on a serving plate; frost with a ½-inch layer of whipped cream mixture. Repeat with remaining cake layers. Frost entire cake with remaining whipped cream mixture, making sure to cover top and sides of cake. Arrange berries on top and sides, pressing firmly into whipped cream mixture. Serve immediately or refrigerate for up to 8 hours. Serves 10.

Lisa Johnson
Hallsville, TX

pick your own

Many strawberry farms now allow you to pick your own strawberries. Try finding one in your area. Most serve up delicious homemade treats such as strawberry ice cream and preserves.

Best-Ever Mud Pie

1 c. sugar
2 eggs, beaten
½ c. margarine, melted and
    cooled slightly
1 t. vanilla extract
⅓ c. all-purpose flour
⅓ c. baking cocoa
¼ t. salt

Optional: 1 c. chopped pecans
    or walnuts
¼ c. hot fudge ice-cream topping
8-oz. container frozen whipped
    topping, thawed
Optional: vanilla or coffee
    ice cream

"This decadent dessert comes together in no time...and it will be eaten up even quicker, I guarantee!"

—Cheryl

Combine sugar, eggs, margarine, vanilla, flour, cocoa and salt in a large bowl; mix well. Stir in nuts, if using; pour into a greased 9" pie plate. Bake at 325 degrees for 25 minutes. Remove from oven and immediately poke holes in the top with a toothpick. Spread fudge topping over pie; cool completely and refrigerate. At serving time, spread whipped topping over pie. Serve with scoops of ice cream, if desired. Serves 6 to 8.

Cheryl Lagler
Zionsville, PA

Chocolate-Peanut Butter Cupcakes

Whip up these cupcakes for any celebration and make them extra special by adding your favorite frosting.

1 T. whipping cream, heated
2 oz. semi-sweet baking
    chocolate, grated
⅔ c. plus 2 t. sugar, divided
¼ c. creamy peanut butter
6 oz. semi-sweet baking
    chocolate

6 T. butter
2 eggs
1 t. vanilla extract
¾ c. all-purpose flour
¼ t. baking soda
¼ t. salt
16-oz. container white frosting

Pour hot cream over 2 ounces grated chocolate and 2 teaspoons sugar in a bowl; stir until combined and chocolate melts. Add peanut butter and mix well; refrigerate 35 to 40 minutes, until slightly firm. Combine 6 ounces chocolate and butter in the top of a double boiler over boiling water; cook over low heat until butter and chocolate melt. Place eggs in a large bowl and beat with an electric mixer at medium speed until foamy; add remaining ⅔ cup sugar and vanilla and beat until fluffy. Add melted chocolate mixture and beat at low speed until mixed. Add flour, baking soda and salt and beat just until combined. Pour batter into lightly greased muffin cups, filling almost ⅔ full. Roll rounded teaspoonfuls of filling into balls and press one ball lightly into the center of each cupcake. Bake at 350 degrees for 15 to 20 minutes. Cool completely before frosting. Makes one dozen.

for a vintage look...

Display cupcakes on a vintage cake stand! Place any that do not fit on the top around the foot of the stand for a sophisticated layered look.

Triple Fudge Cake

3.4-oz. pkg. cook & serve
    chocolate pudding mix
18¼-oz. pkg. chocolate cake
    mix

12-oz. pkg. semi-sweet
    chocolate chips
Optional: vanilla ice cream

"I get requests for this cake all the time, and nothing could be easier to make!"

—Tanya

Prepare pudding according to package directions; stir in cake mix. Spread in a greased 13"x9" baking pan; sprinkle with chocolate chips. Bake at 350 degrees for 35 minutes; cool. Serve with vanilla ice cream, if desired. Serves 12.

Tanya Leach
Adamstown, PA

get crafty!

Invite friends over for an arts and crafts night. Provide materials to decorate holiday items such as pumpkins, ornaments or Valentine cards. Serve a delicious dessert and let the fun begin!

Lone Star Pecan Cake

This rich-tasting cake needs no frosting

1 lb. butter, softened
2 c. sugar
6 eggs, well beaten
1 t. lemon extract
4 c. unbleached all-purpose flour

1½ t. baking powder
4 c. pecan halves
2 c. golden raisins
Optional: powdered sugar

Combine butter and sugar in a large bowl and beat until light and fluffy. Gradually add eggs and lemon extract, beating well. Sift flour and baking powder together 3 times into another large bowl; add nuts and raisins and mix well. Gradually add flour mixture to butter mixture, blending well. Spoon batter into a greased and floured 9" tube pan and bake at 300 degrees for 1½ to 2 hours, until a toothpick inserted near center comes out clean. Cool 15 minutes before removing from pan. When cool, dust with powdered sugar, if desired. Serves 16.

Old-Fashioned Peach Cobbler

Use peaches that aren't overripe so that they'll hold their shape when cooked.

3 c. plus 3 T. all-purpose flour, divided
1 t. salt
1 c. shortening
1½ c. cold water, divided

2 c. sugar
7 c. fresh peaches, peeled, pitted and sliced
½ t. almond extract
½ c. butter, divided

Combine 3 cups flour and salt in a large bowl and mix well; cut in half of shortening until mixture is crumbly. Add remaining shortening and cut in until mixture is consistency of small peas. Sprinkle ½ cup cold water over flour mixture and stir gently with a fork until mixture holds together. Press dough into a smooth ball; divide into thirds. On a lightly floured board, roll out one-third dough to ⅛-inch thickness; cut into 3-inch by one-inch pieces. Place on an ungreased baking sheet and bake at 400 degrees for 8 minutes, or until lightly golden. Cover remaining two-thirds dough with a tea towel and set aside. Combine sugar and remaining 3 tablespoons flour in a large bowl; add peaches, remaining one cup water and almond extract and gently stir to mix. Roll out another one-third of remaining dough to ⅛-inch thickness and fit into bottom and up sides of an ungreased 3-quart casserole dish. Spoon half of peach mixture on top of dough and dot with half of butter. Top with baked pastry strips and remaining peach mixture; dot with remaining butter. Roll out remaining one-third of dough to ⅛-inch thickness, cut into ¾-inch-wide strips and place lattice fashion on top. Trim edges; seal and flute. Bake at 375 degrees for 50 minutes to one hour. Serves 8 to 10.

Karen Moran
Navasota, TX

"I enjoy this cobbler most in the summertime with a big scoop of vanilla ice cream."

—**Karen**

Blackberry-Apple Crunch

This treat tastes especially delicious after a day of blackberry picking!

2¼ c. all-purpose flour, divided
2½ c. sugar, divided
¼ t. salt
1 c. butter, sliced
2½ c. fresh blackberries

4 lbs. Golden Delicious apples,
　peeled, cored and thinly sliced
cinnamon to taste
Optional: vanilla ice cream,
　additional blackberries

Combine 2 cups flour, 1½ cups sugar and salt in a bowl; cut in butter with pastry blender and mix until crumbly. Combine blackberries, apples, remaining ¼ cup flour and remaining sugar in a large bowl; toss to mix and spoon into a greased 13"x9" baking pan. Cover with flour mixture and sprinkle with cinnamon. Bake at 350 degrees for 45 minutes, or until bubbly. Cool slightly before serving. Serve with ice cream and blackberries, if desired. Serves 12.

Blueberry-Lemon Mousse

Lemon and blueberries make a refreshing combination…include a Lemon Crunch Cookie (see page 238) with each serving.

1 qt. fresh blueberries, rinsed
1 c. sugar, divided
5 eggs, separated
½ t. cinnamon

juice of 2 lemons
1 c. whipping cream, whipped
2 t. lemon zest

Combine berries and ¼ cup sugar in a bowl and mix well; refrigerate until ready to use. Beat egg yolks with remaining ¾ cup sugar and cinnamon; add lemon juice and mix well. Pour egg yolk mixture into the top of a double boiler and cook over barely simmering water until mixture is thick enough to coat a spoon, whisking constantly; remove from heat and cool. Beat egg whites until stiff peaks form; fold into egg yolk mixture. Fold in whipped cream and lemon zest. Cover and refrigerate at least one hour. Spoon mousse into serving bowls and top with berry mixture. Serves 8.

make a parfait

Layer mousse, berries and whipped cream in wine or sundae glasses and refrigerate until ready to serve. Provide long spoons so guests can enjoy every last bite.

Tickled-Pink Dessert Drink

An all-occasion pretty-in-pink drink!

1 c. orange juice
½ c. milk
½ c. vanilla yogurt
10-oz. pkg. frozen strawberries,
    thawed

1 t. almond extract
Garnish: one orange, sliced into
    thin wedges

Place orange juice, milk, yogurt, strawberries and almond extract in a blender; cover and blend 40 to 50 seconds, until smooth. Pour into serving glasses; garnish each serving with an orange wedge. Serves 4 to 6.

Raspberry Sorbet

Sorbet is perfect to serve at the end of a long dinner party. It provides a light, fresh finish to a decadent, rich meal.

1 c. sugar
2 c. water
3 pts. fresh raspberries

¼ c. fresh lemon juice
Garnish: whole fresh raspberries,
    fresh mint leaves

Combine sugar and water in a small saucepan and simmer over medium heat 5 minutes; set aside to cool. Place raspberries, cooled syrup and lemon juice in a blender and purée; strain and refrigerate. When chilled, freeze in an ice-cream machine or place in the freezer, stirring occasionally, until soft-frozen. Garnish with whole raspberries and mint leaves. Makes one quart.

Creamsicles

Fresh orange juice makes these creamy frozen treats taste so much better than store-bought.

1 pt. vanilla ice cream or
    ice milk, softened
6-oz. can frozen orange juice
    concentrate, thawed

¼ c. honey
1½ c. fat-free milk
12 craft sticks

Combine ice cream or ice milk, orange juice concentrate and honey in a large bowl; mix well. Gradually beat in fat-free milk and pour into 12 small waxed paper cups or an ice cube tray. Insert sticks into paper cups or ice cube trays when partially frozen. Makes one dozen.

Cinnamon Pancakes in a Jar, page 274
Cider Syrup, page 275

giftable goodies

Show how much you appreciate your hosts by
bringing along some goodies they can enjoy after
the guests are gone. Give them a jump start on
breakfast with Cinnamon Pancakes in a Jar (page
274) or help them kick any dish up a notch with
Cajun Spice Seasoning (page 282). Play to a
sweet tooth with a batch of Crunchy Fudge
(page 300) or S'mores Brownies (page 297)…
a kind gift that makes a lasting impression.

Cinnamon Pancakes in a Jar

(pictured on page 272)

Enjoy with Cider Syrup (page 275), a side of bacon and a good cup of coffee...what a combination!

3 c. all-purpose flour
3 T. sugar
2 T. baking powder

4½ t. cinnamon
1 t. salt

Combine all ingredients in a large bowl and mix well; spoon into a one-quart jar. Secure lid; attach instructions. Makes about 3½ cups.

Instructions:

Combine ¾ cup milk, one egg and 2 tablespoons vegetable oil in a bowl and whisk until well mixed; add 1⅓ cups pancake mix, stirring just until moistened. Pour by ¼ cupfuls into a hot, greased skillet; cook until bubbles form along edge. Flip and cook until both sides are golden. Makes 10.

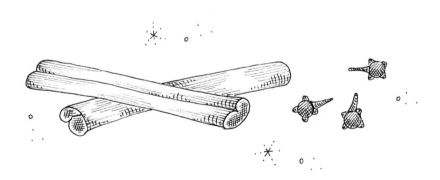

Cider Syrup
(pictured on page 272)

Served over a stack of pancakes or waffles, this makes a yummy addition to any breakfast table.

1 c. sugar	2 c. apple cider
2 T. cornstarch	2 T. lemon juice
½ t. pumpkin pie spice	⅓ c. butter

Combine sugar, cornstarch and pumpkin pie spice in a saucepan; stir in apple cider and lemon juice. Cook over medium heat until mixture comes to a boil and thickens, stirring constantly; boil one minute. Remove from heat and stir in butter. Makes about 2 cups.

Irish Soda Bread

This sweet recipe makes two loaves…one to share, one to enjoy!

4 c. all-purpose flour
1 c. sugar
2 t. baking powder
1 t. baking soda
½ t. salt

3 eggs
2 c. sour cream
1 c. raisins
1 T. caraway seed

Combine flour, sugar, baking powder, baking soda and salt in a large bowl; add eggs and sour cream and mix just until moistened. Fold in raisins; spread batter evenly in 2 greased 8"x4" loaf pans. Sprinkle loaves with caraway seed; bake at 325 degrees for one hour. Makes 2 loaves.

Irish
Soda
Bread

Springtime Pea Soup in a Jar

One taste of this soup will remind you of all the fresh veggies just waiting to sprout in your garden.

16-oz. pkg. split green peas
16-oz. pkg. dried lentils
16-oz. pkg. pearled barley
2 c. elbow macaroni, uncooked
1 c. dried, minced onion

½ c. celery flakes
½ c. dried parsley
2 t. white pepper
1½ t. dried thyme

Combine all ingredients in a large bowl and mix well; spoon into a jar with a tight-fitting lid. Attach instructions. Makes 10 cups.

Instructions:

Combine one cup soup mix with 4 cups seasoned chicken broth in a saucepan; add one cup chopped cooked chicken, if desired. Bring to a boil; reduce heat and simmer 45 minutes to one hour, until peas are tender. Serves 4.

Jambalaya Mix

This easy mix works with lots of combinations...try chicken & sausage or sausage & shrimp.

1 c. long-cooking rice, uncooked
1 T. dried, minced onion
1 T. green pepper flakes
1 T. dried parsley
1 bay leaf

2 t. beef bouillon granules
½ t. garlic powder
½ t. dried thyme
½ t. cayenne pepper

Combine all ingredients in a large bowl and mix well; spoon into a plastic zipping bag. Seal securely; attach instructions.

Instructions:

Combine mix with 3 cups water in a large stockpot; bring to a boil. Reduce heat; add ½ cup diced cooked ham and an 8-ounce can tomato sauce. Simmer 20 minutes. Stir in ½ cup cooked shrimp; cook an additional 5 minutes. Remove from heat; discard bay leaf before serving. Makes 8 cups.

personalized gift tags

Create your own recipe cards to give away with food gifts. Find all kinds of paper tags, stickers, glitter and trims in the scrapbooking aisle of craft stores. Or make a copy of the tag at left, cut out and personalize as you like!

Rosemary Focaccia Mix

Stir up this simple mix as a lovely housewarming present for new neighbors or newlyweds.

1½ c. bread flour	2 t. red pepper flakes
1 env. active dry yeast	1½ t. dried rosemary
1 T. sugar	½ t. salt

Combine all ingredients in a large bowl and mix well; spoon into an airtight container. Seal; attach instructions.

Instructions:

Place mix in a large bowl; add ½ cup very warm water, about 105 to 115 degrees, and 2 tablespoons olive oil. Stir with a wooden spoon until smooth. Add more water, one tablespoonful at a time, if needed to moisten. Knead 8 to 10 times. Place in a greased bowl, turning to coat all sides; cover and let rise until double in bulk. Punch dough down; roll out on a greased jelly-roll pan into a 13-inch by 9-inch rectangle; brush with 2 tablespoons olive oil. Sprinkle with coarse salt to taste; bake at 425 degrees for 5 minutes. Pop any bubbles with a fork; bake an additional 8 minutes. Remove from pan; cut into 3-inch squares. Serves 12.

not your average salt...

Buy specialty sea salts to give with this mix. You can find all sorts of interesting flavors from smoky to spicy or even sweet.

Cajun Spice Seasoning

A Mardi Gras kitchen necessity for any potato, egg or meat dish.

¾ c. salt
¼ c. cayenne pepper
2 T. white pepper
2 T. black pepper

2 T. paprika
2 T. onion powder
2 T. garlic powder
1 t. onion salt

Combine all ingredients in a bowl and mix well; spoon into three ½-cup containers with lids. Store in a cool, dry place. Makes 1½ cups.

Cajun Spice Seasoning

Dad's Favorite Steak Sauce

No need for that catsup bottle when this sauce is in town!

3 T. raspberry jam
2 T. brown sugar, packed
2 T. Worcestershire sauce
2 T. tomato sauce

2 T. malt vinegar
5 drops hot pepper sauce
salt and pepper to taste

Combine all ingredients in a medium saucepan and whisk until well mixed; bring to a boil over high heat. Reduce heat and simmer 10 minutes, or until mixture thickens, stirring frequently. Makes ½ cup.

save 'em for later

Buy steaks when they go on sale and keep them in your freezer until ready to use.

3-Pepper Relish

The perfect garden offering for any cookout host...and a canning recipe that's a snap to make.

1 c. red peppers, minced
1 c. green peppers, minced
1 c. jalapeño peppers, seeded and minced
1 c. cider vinegar (5 percent acidity)

5¼ c. sugar
1 t. butter
1.75-oz. pkg. powdered fruit pectin
6 ½-pt. canning jars and lids, sterilized

Place one cup each red peppers, green peppers and jalapeño peppers in a heavy 6-quart saucepan. Stir in vinegar, sugar and butter; bring mixture to a rolling boil over high heat, stirring constantly. Add pectin and return to a rolling boil over high heat; cook one minute, stirring constantly. Remove from heat and skim off any foam using a metal spoon. Ladle into hot sterilized jars, leaving ¼-inch headspace. Wipe rims; secure lids and rings. Process in a boiling-water bath 15 minutes. Cool 24 hours; check seals. Store properly sealed jars in a cool, dark place and use within 6 months. Refrigerate after opening. Makes 6 jars.

put a lid on it

Host a canning party. Have friends come over to make preserves, jams and relishes. Use the proper canning equipment and then decorate cute jars with ribbons and labels.

Rainbow Popcorn

This is an easy-to-make, fun treat! Use any color food coloring you'd like…orange for Halloween, your team's color or your child's favorite color for a birthday party.

non-stick vegetable spray
8 c. popped popcorn
½ c. milk

2 c. sugar
1 t. vanilla extract
desired food coloring

Completely coat the inside of a large brown paper bag with non-stick vegetable spray. Place popcorn in bag; set aside. Combine milk and sugar in a heavy saucepan and bring to a boil over medium heat, being careful not to let mixture burn; do not scrape the sides of the pan or the sugar will crystallize. Remove from heat. Add vanilla and a few drops of food coloring; mix well. Pour milk mixture over popcorn in bag. Close bag and shake to coat popcorn evenly. Spread popcorn on baking sheets to dry. Store in airtight containers. Makes about 8 cups.

Jill Ball
Highland, UT

"Give away bags of this popcorn as tasty party favors at your next get-together."

—Jill

Oriental Snack Mix

The combination of ingredients in this mix turns simple popcorn into a tasty treat that's impossible to stop eating!

3 T. butter	1 clove garlic, minced
3 T. creamy peanut butter	10 c. popped popcorn
2 t. soy sauce	2 c. chow mein noodles

Combine butter, peanut butter, soy sauce and garlic in a small saucepan over medium-low heat; cook until butter melts and mixture is smooth, stirring constantly. Combine popcorn and chow mein noodles in a large bowl; drizzle with peanut butter mixture. Toss to coat and spread on an ungreased jelly-roll pan. Bake at 300 degrees for 10 to 15 minutes, stirring after 5 minutes; cool and store in an airtight container. Makes about 12 cups.

Away-Game Snack Mix

Take these spicy munchies anywhere!

1 t. chili powder
½ t. onion powder
½ t. garlic powder
½ t. kosher salt
⅛ t. cayenne pepper

2 qts. popped popcorn
2 c. mini pretzels
2 c. bite-size crispy corn cereal
    squares, toasted

Combine seasonings in a small bowl; set aside. Gently toss popcorn, pretzels and cereal in a large mixing bowl; sprinkle with seasonings. Toss again; store in an airtight container. Serves 12.

pack like a pro

Pour snack mix into lightweight, wide-mouth sports bottles. They're easy to tote and can be used again and again!

Carrot Cake Mix

Place in an Easter basket along with a can of crushed pineapple and a large bunch of carrots…tie it all up in green cellophane.

3 c. all-purpose flour
2 c. sugar
2 t. vanilla powder
2 t. baking soda

½ c. chopped pecans
2 t. cinnamon
¼ t. nutmeg

Combine all ingredients in a large bowl; mix well. Spoon into an airtight container; attach instructions.

Instructions:

Place mix in a large bowl; add 1½ cups vegetable oil, 3 eggs, 3 cups grated carrots and an 8-ounce can crushed pineapple. Blend until smooth; spread in a greased 13"x9" baking pan. Bake at 350 degrees for 40 to 50 minutes, until a toothpick inserted near center comes out clean. Cool. Serves 15.

Banana-Bran Muffin Mix

Make several bags at once…you'll be glad to have them on hand when guests stop by for a visit!

1 c. all-purpose flour
1 c. whole bran
3 T. sugar

2½ t. baking powder
1 t. salt

Combine all ingredients in a bowl and mix well. Spoon into a plastic zipping bag; seal. Attach instructions.

Instructions:

Place mix in a large bowl; add one beaten egg, one cup mashed bananas, ¼ cup milk and 2 tablespoons vegetable oil. Stir just until moistened; fill greased or paper-lined muffin cups ⅔ full with batter. Bake at 400 degrees for 20 to 25 minutes. Makes one dozen.

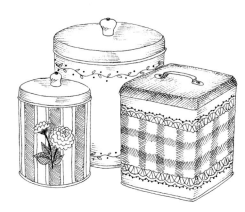

think outside the box

Find various types of containers at your local arts and crafts store. Use large Mason jars, antique cookie cans or decorated square tins to spice things up.

Tea Cookies in a Jar

A cup of tea, a plate of warm cookies…what more could you want?

1½ c. all-purpose flour
1 t. baking soda
1 t. cinnamon
½ t. nutmeg
½ t. salt

2 c. long-cooking oats, uncooked
¾ c. brown sugar, packed
½ c. sugar
¾ c. raisins

Combine flour, baking soda, cinnamon, nutmeg and salt in a bowl and mix well; spoon into a one-quart, wide-mouth jar. Pack firmly; layer remaining ingredients except raisins in order listed, packing each layer. Spoon raisins into a plastic zipping bag. Secure lid on jar; tie on bag of raisins and instructions.

Instructions:

Empty mix and raisins into a large bowl; toss gently to blend. Add ¾ cup softened butter, one beaten egg and one teaspoon vanilla extract; mix well. Shape into one-inch balls; arrange 2 inches apart on parchment paper-lined baking sheets. Bake at 350 degrees for 10 to 12 minutes; cool on baking sheets 5 minutes. Remove to wire racks to cool completely. Makes 3 dozen.

Whoopie Pies

2¼ c. all-purpose flour
½ c. baking cocoa
1½ t. baking soda
1¼ t. cream of tartar
1¼ c. sugar

⅔ c. shortening
2 eggs
1 t. vanilla extract
1 c. milk

Combine flour, baking cocoa, baking soda and cream of tartar in a bowl; mix well and set aside. Combine sugar and shortening in a large bowl and beat until fluffy; add eggs and vanilla and mix well. Alternately add flour mixture and milk, blending just until combined. Drop by tablespoonfuls onto greased baking sheets; bake at 350 degrees for 8 to 10 minutes. Remove from baking sheets and cool on wire racks. Spread heaping tablespoonfuls of Filling on flat sides of half the cookies; top each with another cookie, making a sandwich. Wrap in plastic wrap; freeze until firm. Makes about 2½ dozen.

Filling:

5 T. all-purpose flour
1 c. milk
1 c. shortening
½ c. butter, softened

1 c. sugar
¼ t. salt
1½ t. vanilla extract

Combine flour and milk in a small saucepan; cook over medium heat until thickened, stirring constantly. Cool to room temperature. Combine shortening, butter, sugar, salt and vanilla in a large bowl; beat with an electric mixer at medium speed until well mixed. Add milk mixture; beat until light and fluffy.

S'mores Brownies

18¼-oz. pkg. brownie mix
3 c. mini marshmallows
4 whole graham crackers,
   coarsely broken

2 1.55-oz. chocolate candy bars,
   broken into small pieces

Prepare and bake brownie mix in a greased 8"x8" baking pan according to package directions. Remove pan from oven and immediately sprinkle brownies with marshmallows and graham cracker pieces. Broil 30 to 60 seconds, until marshmallows are golden, watching carefully because marshmallows brown quickly. Immediately sprinkle with candy bar pieces. Cool 15 minutes before cutting into squares; serve warm. Makes 16.

Abi Buening
Grand Forks, ND

"These are so gooey and delicious! They are a terrific way to use up leftover Halloween candy bars, but sometimes I use chocolate chips instead."

—Abi

Batch-for-a-Bunch Cookies

A class of 22, a team of 12…let the number you need determine the cookies' size!

½ c. sugar
½ c. brown sugar, packed
⅓ c. margarine, softened
⅓ c. shortening
1 egg
½ t. baking soda

½ t. salt
1½ t. vanilla extract
1½ c. all-purpose flour
½ c. chopped nuts
1 c. semi-sweet chocolate chips

Combine sugar, brown sugar, margarine, shortening, egg, baking soda, salt and vanilla in a large bowl; mix well. Add flour and blend just until mixed. Fold in nuts and chips; drop by spoonfuls onto ungreased baking sheets. Bake at 375 degrees for 12 to 13 minutes. Makes 2 to 3 dozen.

Terri Childress
Staunton, VA

Oatmeal Crispies

This old-fashioned recipe is very versatile...add raisins or chocolate chips, bake big or small. Any way you make them, everyone will love them!

1 c. shortening
1 c. sugar
1 c. brown sugar, packed
2 eggs, beaten
1 t. vanilla extract
1½ c. all-purpose flour

1 t. salt
1 t. baking soda
3 c. quick-cooking oats, uncooked
½ c. walnuts, chopped

Combine shortening, sugar and brown sugar in a large bowl; mix well. Add eggs and vanilla; mix well. Add flour, salt and baking soda and mix well. Stir in oats and walnuts. Shape dough into logs; wrap in wax paper and refrigerate until chilled or overnight. Slice ¼-inch thick and place on ungreased baking sheets; bake at 350 degrees for 10 minutes. Makes 3 dozen.

Susan Miller

cookie stash

Want to save these for a rainy day? Cookies freeze very well. Store in an airtight container with parchment paper dividing the layers. Label and freeze for up to one month.

Crunchy Fudge

Fudge is always a welcome indulgence…a great gift for friends!

4 c. sugar
1 c. evaporated milk
½ c. corn syrup

6 T. butter
1 t. vanilla extract

Combine sugar, evaporated milk, corn syrup and butter in a heavy saucepan; heat over medium-low heat until sugar dissolves. Increase heat to medium; heat to boiling, stirring occasionally. Heat, without stirring, to the soft-ball stage, or 234 to 240 degrees on a candy thermometer; remove from heat. Place pan in a 1½-inch deep cold water bath; add vanilla, without stirring. Let cool to 100 degrees; remove from water bath. Blend until fudge thickens and loses its gloss; spread evenly in 2 buttered 8"x8" baking pans. Pour Topping on top; cool. Cut into squares to serve. Makes 3⅓ pounds.

Topping:

1 c. sugar
¼ c. water
¼ c. butter

2 T. evaporated milk
1 t. vanilla extract
1 c. chopped pecans, toasted

Stir sugar and water together in a small skillet; heat over medium-high heat until sugar dissolves. Increase heat to high; stir until mixture turns golden. Remove from heat; carefully add butter, evaporated milk and vanilla, stirring to mix. Add pecans; stir to coat.

"Congratulations!" Caramel Squares

Wrap these special treats individually and place them in a graduation cap…don't forget to add a diploma declaring "Great job, graduate!"

1½ c. brown sugar, packed
    and divided
½ c. margarine, softened
2 eggs, separated

1½ c. all-purpose flour
2 t. baking powder
1 t. vanilla extract
¼ c. chopped nuts

Double or triple the recipe to give away to all your friends and neighbors.

Combine ½ cup brown sugar, margarine, egg yolks, flour, baking powder and vanilla in a large bowl; mix well. Press into a greased 8"x8" baking pan; set aside. Place egg whites in a separate bowl and whisk until stiff peaks form; gradually blend in remaining one cup brown sugar. Spread over crust; sprinkle with nuts. Bake at 325 degrees for 25 minutes, or until golden. Cool; cut into squares. Makes 1½ dozen.

Lemon Chess Bars

These delicious bars freeze well...keep some on hand to serve to unexpected guests!

½ c. butter or margarine, softened

1 c. plus 2 T. all-purpose flour, sifted and divided

¼ c. powdered sugar

2 eggs

1 c. sugar

zest of 1 lemon

3 T. lemon juice

additional powdered sugar

Place butter or margarine in a bowl and beat with an electric mixer at medium speed until fluffy. Add one cup flour and ¼ cup powdered sugar and beat well; spoon into an ungreased 8"x8" pan and press firmly. Bake at 325 degrees for 20 minutes. Meanwhile, combine eggs, sugar, remaining 2 tablespoons flour, lemon zest and lemon juice in a bowl and mix well; pour over baked bottom layer. Bake 25 more minutes or until center is set. Cool. Sprinkle with powdered sugar. Cut into bars. Makes 16.

Arlynn Geers

Orange Float Mix

A yummy warm-weather treat that you can share year 'round.

4 c. powdered milk
2 c. unsweetened orange drink
  mix

1 c. sugar
3-oz. pkg. powdered egg whites

Combine all ingredients in a large bowl; mix well. Spoon into an airtight container; store in a cool, dry place and use within 6 months. Attach instructions. Makes 8 cups.

Instructions:

Place ½ cup mix and one cup water in a blender; add 2 to 3 ice cubes. Process until well blended; serve immediately. Serves one.

orange
float
soda

16 memorable menus

sunrise brunch

serves 6

orange juice

Potato & Ham Frittata (page 67)*

Ginger-Lime Salad (page 161)*

Cinnamon-Apple Muffins (page 227)

seafood fest

serves 4

Chive & Dijon Crab Cakes (page 50)

Louisiana Shrimp Boil (page 54)

Summer Vegetable Salad (page 160)**

Lemon Crunch Cookies (page 238)

* denotes double recipe
** denotes half recipe

ladies' luncheon

serves 6

Fruity Spiced Tea (page 12)

Chunky Gazpacho (page 122)*

Dilly Egg Salad Sandwiches (page 141)*

Cherry Macaroons (page 234)

afternoon tea

serves 12

hot tea

Rosemary-Lemon Scones (page 220)*

English Crumpets (page 225)

*Cinnamon-Sugar Butter Cookies
(page 236)*

game night

serves 8

Slow-Cooker Pub Beer Dip (page 25)

Cheesy Chili Bake (page 116)*

Grilled Garlic Burgers (page 81)*

Hello Dolly Bars (page 244)

simply Italian

serves 6

Italian Bread (page 198)

Minestrone Soup (page 133)

Easy Cheesy Manicotti (page 46)

Garlicky Spinach (page 175)

* denotes double recipe

community cookout

serves 10 to 12

Citrus Slush (page 14)

*Slow-Cooker Pulled Pork Sandwiches
(page 153)*

Three-Bean Basil Salad (page 162)

Old-Fashioned Peach Cobbler (page 263)

dinner on the patio

serves 6

Country Apple Sipper (page 10)

Apricot-Glazed Pork Chops (page 68)*

Country-Time Green Beans (page 180)

Sweet Potato Casserole (page 189)

Blackberry-Apple Crunch (page 264)

Southwestern fiesta

serves 6

Homemade Guacamole (page 22)

Southwestern Casserole (page 115)

Chili-Rubbed Steaks (page 74)

Dulce de Leche Bars (page 241)

Sunday supper

serves 6

*Slow-Cooker Farmhouse Pot Roast
(page 78)*

Country Biscuits Supreme (page 213)

Best-Ever Mud Pie (page 257)

*denotes double recipe

lunch in the garden

serves 8

Cheesy Fruit and Nut Spread (page 26)

Ranch Chicken Wraps (page 147)

Marinated Sugar Snap Peas (page 172)

*Chewy Chocolate Chip Cookies
(page 240)*

weekend playdate

serves 8

Pizza Roll Snacks (page 37)

Macaroni & Cheese (page 85)

Dressed-Up Dogs (page 150)*

*Chocolate-Peanut Butter Cupcakes
(page 258)*

portable picnic

serves 6

Buttermilk Fried Chicken (page 61)

Icebox Slaw (page 164)

Super-Fast Scalloped Potatoes (page 191)

Mini Apple Hand Pies (page 250)

Latin lunch

serves 4

Refreshing Citrus Blush (page 15)

Lisa's Chicken Tortilla Soup (page 130)

Black Bean Burgers (page 142)

Creamsicles (page 270)

* denotes double recipe

backyard barbecue

serves 8

Spiced Lemonade (page 11)*

Barbecued Baby Back Ribs (page 71)*

Speedy Baked Beans (page 182)

Overnight Oriental Salad (page 167)

soup buffet

serves 6 to 8

Dan's Broccoli & Cheese Soup (page 127)

Italian Sausage Soup (page 132)

Chicken Gumbo (page 129)

Rosemary Crisp Bread (page 205)

METRIC EQUIVALENTS

The recipes that appear in this cookbook use the standard U.S. method for measuring liquid and dry or solid ingredients (teaspoons, tablespoons and cups). The information in the following charts is provided to help cooks outside the United States successfully use these recipes. All equivalents are approximate.

METRIC EQUIVALENTS FOR DIFFERENT TYPES OF INGREDIENTS

A standard cup measure of a dry or solid ingredient will vary in weight depending on the type of ingredient.
A standard cup of liquid is the same volume for any type of liquid. Use the following chart when converting standard cup measures to grams (weight) or milliliters (volume).

Standard Cup	Fine Powder (ex. flour)	Grain (ex. rice)	Granular (ex. sugar)	Liquid Solids (ex. butter)	Liquid (ex. milk)
1	140 g	150 g	190 g	200 g	240 ml
¾	105 g	113 g	143 g	150 g	180 ml
⅔	93 g	100 g	125 g	133 g	160 ml
½	70 g	75 g	95 g	100 g	120 ml
⅓	47 g	50 g	63 g	67 g	80 ml
¼	35 g	38 g	48 g	50 g	60 ml
⅛	18 g	19 g	24 g	25 g	30 ml

USEFUL EQUIVALENTS FOR LIQUID INGREDIENTS BY VOLUME

¼ tsp =				1 ml
½ tsp =				2 ml
1 tsp =				5 ml
3 tsp =	1 Tbsp	= ½ fl oz =	15 ml
	2 Tbsp = ⅛ cup	= 1 fl oz =	30 ml
	4 Tbsp = ¼ cup	= 2 fl oz =	60 ml
	5⅓ Tbsp = ⅓ cup	= 3 fl oz =	80 ml
	8 Tbsp = ½ cup	= 4 fl oz =	120 ml
	10⅔ Tbsp = ⅔ cup	= 5 fl oz =	160 ml
	12 Tbsp = ¾ cup	= 6 fl oz =	180 ml
	16 Tbsp = 1 cup	= 8 fl oz =	240 ml
1 pt =	2 cups =	16 fl oz =	480 ml
1 qt =	4 cups =	32 fl oz =	960 ml
		33 fl oz =	1000 ml = 1 liter

USEFUL EQUIVALENTS FOR DRY INGREDIENTS BY WEIGHT

(To convert ounces to grams, multiply the number of ounces by 30.)

1 oz	=	¹⁄₁₆ lb	=	30 g
4 oz	=	¼ lb	=	120 g
8 oz	=	½ lb	=	240 g
12 oz	=	¾ lb	=	360 g
16 oz	=	1 lb	=	480 g

USEFUL EQUIVALENTS FOR LENGTH

(To convert inches to centimeters, multiply the number of inches by 2.5.)

1 in =		= 2.5 cm	
6 in =	½ ft	= 15 cm	
12 in =	1 ft	= 30 cm	
36 in =	3 ft = 1 yd =	90 cm	
40 in =		= 100 cm = 1 meter	

USEFUL EQUIVALENTS FOR COOKING/OVEN TEMPERATURES

	Fahrenheit	Celsius	Gas Mark
Freeze Water	32° F	0° C	
Room Temperature	68° F	20° C	
Boil Water	212° F	100° C	
Bake	325° F	160° C	3
	350° F	180° C	4
	375° F	190° C	5
	400° F	200° C	6
	425° F	220° C	7
	450° F	230° C	8
Broil			Grill

index

frostings, fillings & toppings

Our Story

Back in 1984 we were next-door neighbors raising our families in the little town of Delaware, Ohio. We were two moms with small children looking for a way to do what we loved and stay home with the kids too. We shared a love of home cooking and making memories with family & friends. After many a conversation over the backyard fence, **Gooseberry Patch** was born.

We put together the first catalog & cookbooks at our kitchen tables and packed boxes from the basement, enlisting the help of our loved ones wherever we could. From that little family, we've grown to include an amazing group of creative folks who love cooking, decorating and creating as much as we do.

Hard to believe it's been more than 25 years since those kitchen-table days. Today we're best known for our homestyle, family-friendly cookbooks. We love hand-picking the recipes and are tickled to share our inspiration, ideas and more with you. Our hope is that each book captures the stories and heart of all of you who have shared with us. Whether you've been along for the ride from the beginning or are just discovering us, welcome to our family!

Your friends at Gooseberry Patch

We couldn't make our best-selling cookbooks without YOU!

Each of our books is filled with recipes from cooks just like you, gathered from kitchens all across the country.

Share your tried & true recipes with us on our website and you could be selected for an upcoming cookbook. If your recipe is included, you'll receive a FREE copy of the cookbook when it's published!

www.gooseberrypatch.com

We'd love to add YOU to our Circle of Friends!

Get free recipes, crafts, giveaways and so much more when you join our email club...join us online at all the spots below for even more goodies!